LEARN ABOUT

A LEARNING AND ACTIVITY BOOK

Color your own guide to the birds that wing their way across the plains, hills, forests, deserts, and mountains of Texas.

TEXAS BIRDS

Text by **MARK W. LOCKWOOD**,
    Conservation Biologist, Natural Resource Program

Editorial Direction by **GEORG ZAPPLER**

Art Direction by **ELENA T. IVY**

Educational Consultants **JULIANN POOL** and **BEVERLY MORRELL**

Another *Learn About Texas* publication from

 UNIVERSITY OF TEXAS PRESS, AUSTIN

Copyright © 1997 by Texas Parks and Wildlife Press
First University of Texas Press edition, 2007
All rights reserved
Printed in the United States of America
Originally published by Texas Parks and Wildlife Press

ISBN 978-0-292-71685-8

Requests for permission to reproduce material from this work should be sent to Permissions, University of Texas Press, P.O. Box 7819, Austin, TX 78713-7819
www.utexas.edu/utpress/about/bpermission.html
∞ The paper used in this book meets the minimum requirements of ANSI / NISO Z39.48-1992 (R1997) (Permanence of Paper).

2006939525

Key to the Cover

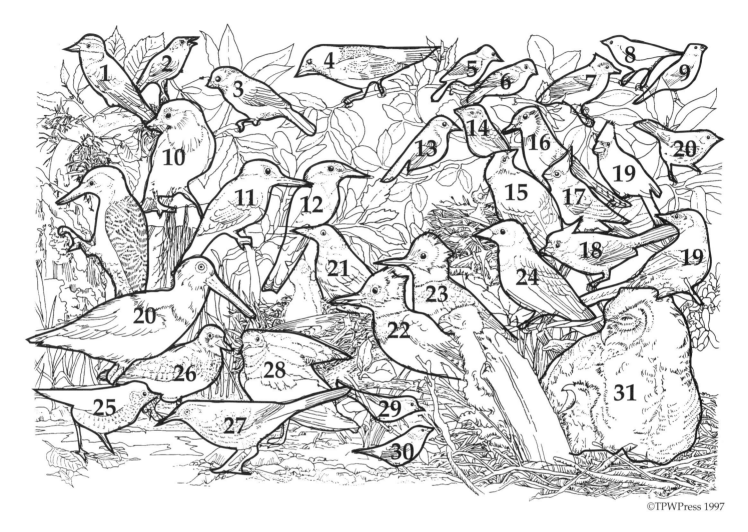

©TPWPress 1997

1 Great Kiskadee
2 Carolina Wren
3 Carolina Chickadee
4 Altamira Oriole
5 Black-capped Vireo ♀
6 Black-capped Vireo ♂
7 Tufted Titmouse
8 Painted Bunting
9 Indigo Bunting
10 Green Jay
11 Green Kingfisher ♀
12 Green Kingfisher ♂
13 Vermillion Flycatcher ♂
14 Vermillion Flycatcher ♀
15 Blue Jay

16 Blue Jay ♀
17 Pyrrhuloxia ♀
18 Pyrrhuloxia ♂
19 Northern Cardinal
20 Ovenbird
21 Brown Thrasher
22 Belted Kingfisher ♂
23 Belted Kingfisher ♀
24 Scissor-tailed Flycatcher
25 Wood Thrush
26 Ruddy Turnstone
27 Long-billed Thrasher
28 Killdeer
29 Olive Sparrow ♂
30 Olive Sparrow ♀
31 Great Horned Owl

♀ =female   ♂ =male

Texas Birds

More kinds of birds have been found in Texas than any other state in the United States: just over 600 species. One of the main reasons Texas has so many birds is its location. Texas is in the southern part of the United States and it is also in the center of the continent. This central location means that birds from both the eastern and western U.S. can be seen in Texas. Texas also shares a long border with Mexico and as a result we have many species of birds that are found primarily in Mexico.

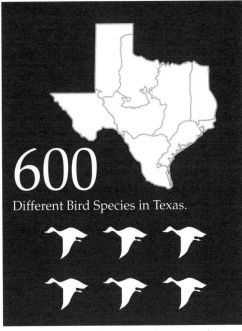

600 Different Bird Species in Texas.

Mark an "X" on the map where you live.

900 Different Bird Species in North America.

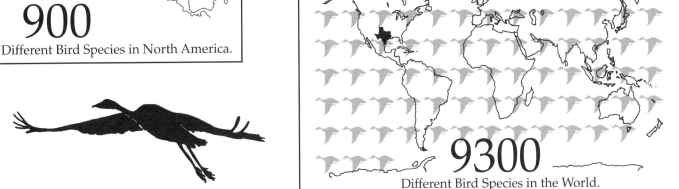

9300 Different Bird Species in the World.

Texas birds can be grouped into four major categories: **summer residents**, **winter residents**, **permanent residents**, and **migrants**.

- **Summer residents** come to Texas during the nesting season, usually from the south. Some of these arrive in Texas as early as March and may leave as early as July.
- **Winter residents** generally are found farther north during the nesting season and migrate south to Texas to spend the winter.

  (There are birds that are summer residents in some areas of Texas and winter residents in others.)
- **Permanent residents** are birds that spend the entire year in part or all of Texas. Some birds are present all year, but actually consist of two populations. The summer resident population migrates south in the winter as birds of the same species move into Texas from up north for the winter.
- **Migrants** are species that only pass through Texas on their way north and south as part of their migration. Most of these are **neotropical migrants**, meaning that they come from the New World tropics. These birds spend the winter in the tropical climate of Central and South America and then migrate back to the temperate climates of the United States and Canada. Many of our summer residents are also neotropical migrants.
- **Accidentals** are birds that don't fit into any of these major categories. These birds are far from where they naturally occur and they got to Texas by sheer accident.

Taxonomy

Scientists have developed a **system** in which all living things (organisms) can be placed and then given a scientific name. This system is called **taxonomy** and it consists of "higher" and "lower" groups. The higher the group, the more broad it is – meaning that it contains a wider range of organisms than the group below it. Let's see how this system works for, let's say, the Bald Eagle.

To fit this organism into the topmost level, we need to place it into one of five divisions called **kingdoms**. Animals, plants, fungi, bacteria and one-celled organisms each have their own kingdom. The Bald Eagle is obviously an animal, hence it belongs in the Kingdom Animalia (Latin for "animal").

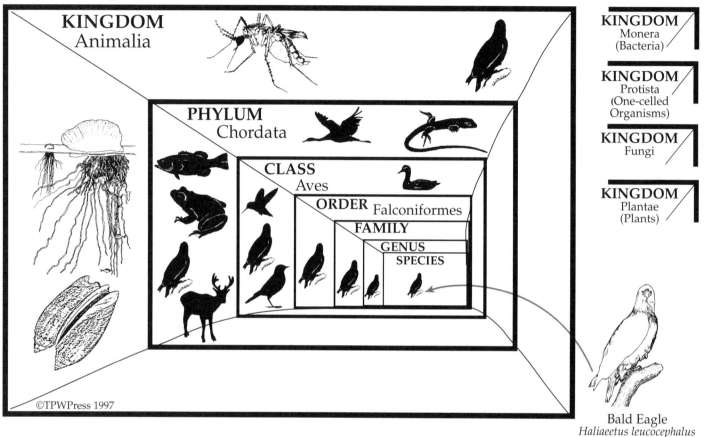

©TPWPress 1997

Bald Eagle
Haliaeetus leucocephalus

    KINGDOM ANIMALIA (ah-nee-mah-lee-ah) contains: coelenterates (jellyfsh, etc.), echinoderms (starfish, etc.) flatworms, segmented worms, mollusks, jointed-legged animals (insects, etc.), ***backboned animals***. The level below the kingdom is that of the **phylum**. Among animals, birds belong with the chordates (called Chordata in Latin) which include all the backboned animals.

    PHYLUM CHORDATA (kor-dah-tah) contains: backboned animals — fishes, amphibians, reptiles, ***birds***, mammals. The next level down is that of the **class**. Among chordates, birds have their own class called Aves (Latin for "birds").

    CLASS AVES (ay-vees) contains: ostriches, penguins, cranes, pelicans, storks, geese and ducks, ***birds of prey***, shorebirds, game birds, gulls, pigeons, parrots, owls, swifts, woodpeckers, perching birds. On the level below the class is the **order**. There are 27 orders of birds. Eagles, together with other birds of prey, belong in the order Falconiformes (which means "shaped like a falcon").

    ORDER FALCONIFORMES (fall-ko-nee-for-mees) contains: ***eagles, hawks, kites***, the Secretary Bird. Below the level of order comes the grouping called the **family**. Eagles, together with hawks and kites (but not the Secretary Bird), are placed in the family Accipitridae (meaning "hawks" in Latin).

    FAMILY ACCIPITRIDAE (axee-pitt-ree-day) contains: ***eagles***, hawks, kites. Below the family level is the level of the **genus** (plural genera). The genus is a group of very closely related species. The genus that contains the Bald Eagle of North America as well as the White-tailed Eagle of Eurasia is called **Haliaeetus**, meaning "sea-eagle." (Other kinds of eagles belong to several other genera.)

    GENUS HALIAEETUS (hally-eh-eetus) contains: ***Bald Eagle***, White-tailed Eagle. Each genus usually contains several **species**, the lowest level in taxonomic classification. It is at the species level that an organism gets its scientific name which always contains two parts. The first part is the genus name and the second is the name of the species in that genus. Both names are usually italicized, with the genus spelled with a capital. In the case of the Bald Eagle, its species name is leucocephalus (meaning "white-head"). The full scientific name is therefore *Haliaeetus leucocephalus*.

    SPECIES HALIAEETUS LEUCOCEPHALUS (lew-koh-sefa-luss) contains only the Bald Eagle.

Ecological Regions of Texas

Texas is roughly 800 miles across from east to west and a little more than 800 miles from the north to the south. Not only is Texas a big state, but it is also one of contrasts. Elevations range from over 8,000 feet in the mountains of the west to sea level along the Gulf coast. As you travel from east to west in Texas, it becomes drier. The average rainfall for a year ranges from about 56 inches in the southeastern part of the state to just eight inches in far West Texas. These differences from region to region have resulted in a wide variety of habitats.

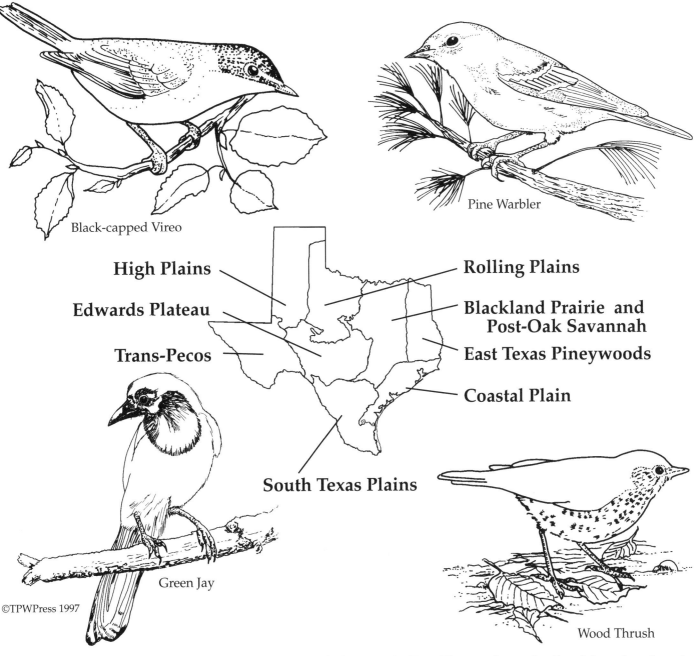

Black-capped Vireo

Pine Warbler

High Plains

Edwards Plateau

Trans-Pecos

Rolling Plains

Blackland Prairie and Post-Oak Savannah

East Texas Pineywoods

Coastal Plain

South Texas Plains

Green Jay

©TPWPress 1997

Wood Thrush

There are large areas of Texas that have similar habitats. In East Texas, along the Louisiana border, the habitat is primarily a pine forest, but as you go west and the land becomes more arid, or dry, the forests become grasslands and finally those grasslands become desert. Areas with similar habitats are often referred to as ecological regions or ecoregions. Each of these regions is very different from the others and each has a few special birds that are not found in any other area of Texas. These birds may be adapted for the overall habitat in which they live or they may be so specialized that they have to be around a certain plant. But, there are also birds that are not restricted to a certain area of the state and can be found in all of the ecoregions.

Symbols Used for Field Notes

About . . . Geographic Range

 You might live in a wet and humid forested area or in a dry desert region. You could be in the cold north or the warm south.

 Birds live in all of the different ecological regions of Texas. You can find birds in forests, marshes, grasslands and deserts as well as up in the mountains and in the lowlands along the coast.

About . . . Nesting Place

 Your house might be on a hill or along a river. It could be on a busy street or along a quiet country road.

 Birds make their nests in all kinds of places, from nests on the ground to nests placed high up on trees or on cliffs.

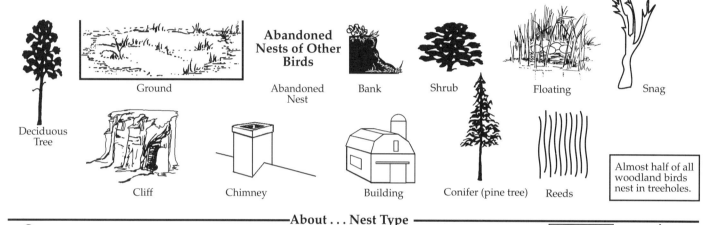

Deciduous Tree   Ground   Abandoned Nests of Other Birds   Abandoned Nest   Bank   Shrub   Floating   Snag

Cliff   Chimney   Building   Conifer (pine tree)   Reeds

Almost half of all woodland birds nest in treeholes.

About . . . Nest Type

 You could be living in a little shack or a big house or in a tent or a cabin.

Some bird nests are shaped like cups, while others resemble saucers. And sometimes the nest is just a tree cavity or a hole in the ground.

Platform   Scrape   Saucer   Burrow   Cup   Cavity   Pendant   Sphere

About . . . Favorite Food

 What is your favorite food? Is it fish, salad or pizza? Well, birds have preferences, too, depending on whether they are birds of prey or seed-eating sparrows.

 Birds' diets are as varied as their physical appearance. Food preferences range from catching other birds in flight to fishing to pecking for seeds on the ground.

Fish   Small Mammals   Insects   Fruit   Seeds   Aquatic Invertebrates   Greens   Birds

About . . . What They Like To Eat

Purple Martins can easily eat 2,000 mosquitoes a day.

A Northern Flicker makes a snack of 5,000 ants.

Scarlet Tanagers can eat 35 harmful Gypsy Moth larvae a minute.

The Mourning Dove eats seeds, like ragweed seeds, and can eat 9,000 in one meal.

Remember you can make up your own symbols for your journal.

©TPWPress 1997

Field Notes for the Great Blue Heron

Range   Nesting Place   Nest Type   Favorite Food
Size: Length 38", Wingspan 70"

Upperparts & neck: slate gray
Head: white
Bill: yellow
Underparts: dark
Legs: yellowish

True or False?
A bird that hatches with its eyes open, is covered with down and leaves the nest within two days is called precocial.

Did You Know That . . .
The English name "heron" for this kind of a long-legged, long-necked bird goes back to about 800 years ago.

Herons are considered semi-altricial. That means that when they hatch they can't leave the nest or feed themselves, yet their eyes are open and they are covered with down.

True or False?
A bird that hatches naked, helpless, and with its eyes closed is called altricial.

Great Blue Heron

The Great Blue Heron is the largest heron found in Texas. It can be seen throughout the state wherever fish and frogs, its favorite food items, are available. Herons can be told from cranes in flight by the way they hold their necks. Herons fly with their necks folded over their shoulders, while cranes hold their necks straight out.

Living Dinosaurs?

What sets birds apart from all the other backboned animals (the vertebrates) are their feathers. The earliest fossil vertebrate, found together with unquestionable feather impressions in the rock that contains the bones, is called *Archaeopteryx*. It comes from Germany and it is dated to about 150 million years ago.

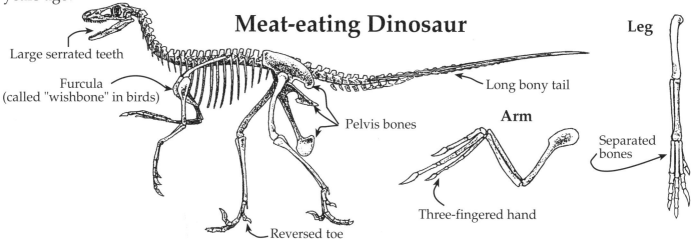

Meat-eating Dinosaur

Large serrated teeth

Furcula (called "wishbone" in birds)

Long bony tail

Pelvis bones

Reversed toe

Arm

Three-fingered hand

Leg

Separated bones

The skeleton of *Archaeopteryx* is so strikingly similar to that of the small meat-eating dinosaurs that fossil experts believe that dinosaurs and birds are closely related. Some even think that birds are directly descended from dinosaurs and could be called living dinosaurs.

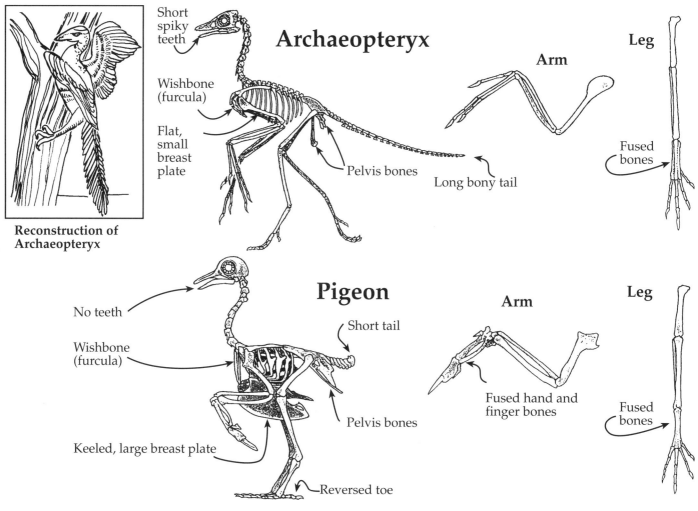

Reconstruction of Archaeopteryx

Archaeopteryx

Short spiky teeth

Wishbone (furcula)

Flat, small breast plate

Pelvis bones

Long bony tail

Arm

Leg

Fused bones

Pigeon

No teeth

Wishbone (furcula)

Keeled, large breast plate

Short tail

Pelvis bones

Reversed toe

Arm

Fused hand and finger bones

Leg

Fused bones

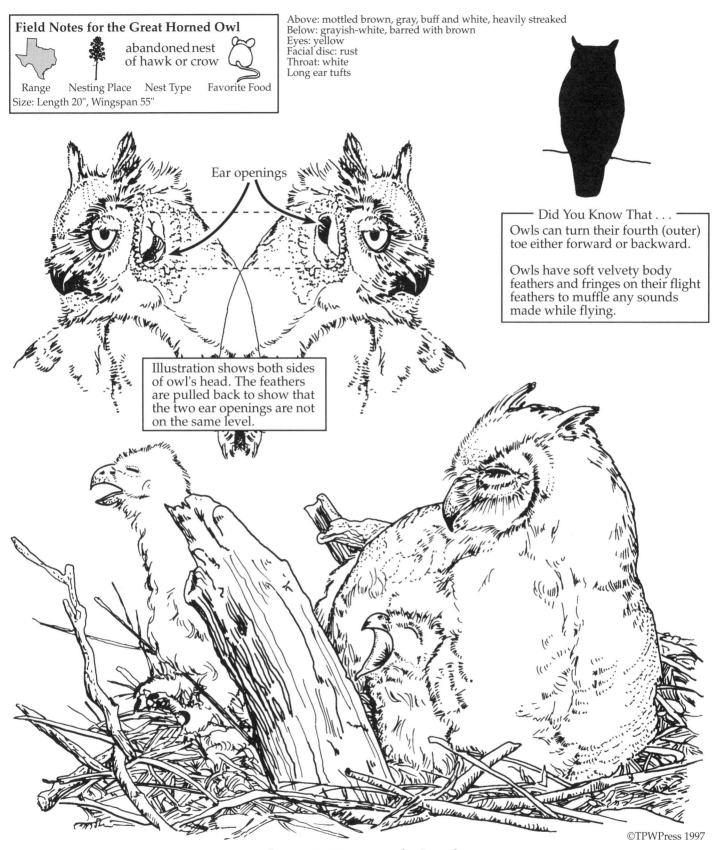

Field Notes for the Great Horned Owl

Range   Nesting Place   Nest Type   Favorite Food
abandoned nest of hawk or crow
Size: Length 20", Wingspan 55"

Above: mottled brown, gray, buff and white, heavily streaked
Below: grayish-white, barred with brown
Eyes: yellow
Facial disc: rust
Throat: white
Long ear tufts

Ear openings

Illustration shows both sides of owl's head. The feathers are pulled back to show that the two ear openings are not on the same level.

— Did You Know That . . . —
Owls can turn their fourth (outer) toe either forward or backward.

Owls have soft velvety body feathers and fringes on their flight feathers to muffle any sounds made while flying.

©TPWPress 1997

Great Horned Owl

The Great Horned Owl is the largest species of owl in Texas. The ear openings of an owl face forward on the head and they are not symmetrical. In other words, they are not at the same level on each side of the head. This allows an owl to pinpoint the exact spot from which the sound comes. The owl's facial disc, formed by a ruff of stiff feathers, helps funnel sound to its ears.

What makes up a Bird?

External Features

When trying to identify birds, it is important to know the names given to different parts of the body, since bird colors and patterns vary from head to tail and from the back to the belly.

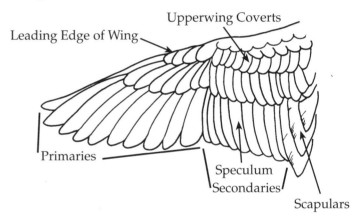

Crown
Eye ring
Forehead
Bill
Lore
Chin
Throat
Chest
Breast
Wing Bars
Belly
Flank
Nape (Collar)
Back
Rump
Upper Tail Coverts
Outer Tail Feathers
Under Tail Coverts (Crissum)
Tarsus

Feathers

The **long feathers** of a bird (that is, its wing and tail feathers) have a strong central shaft that carries interlocking feather barbs on each side. In addition to long feathers, birds also have a layer of shorter **contour** or **body feathers** covering their bodies, and a lining of fluffy feathers called **down** located mostly on their undersides.

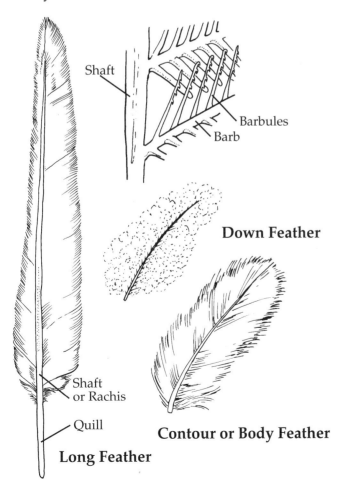

Shaft
Barbules
Barb
Down Feather
Shaft or Rachis
Quill
Contour or Body Feather
Long Feather

Wing from above

Upperwing Coverts
Leading Edge of Wing
Primaries
Speculum
Secondaries
Scapulars

Wing from below

Wrist
Underwing Coverts
Axillars
Primaries
Wing Lining
Secondaries
Trailing Edge of Wing

Feather Color
The colors of bird feathers are produced in two ways. One is by chemical pigments laid down in the feather when it is being formed. The other is by the structure of the feathers determining how they reflect light.

Looking after the Feathers
To preen its feathers, a bird draws each feather carefully through its bill. This action fits the barbs and barbules back into place. Preening also removes parasites.

Field Notes for the Killdeer

Range   Nesting Place   Nest Type   Favorite Food

Size: Length 8", Wingspan 20"

Back & head: brown
Forehead, chin & collar: white
Eye ring: orange
Underparts: white
Legs: pale
Upper tail & lower back: orange
Adult: two black neckbands
Juvenile: only one neckband

What's a "brood patch"?

Most birds develop a "brood patch" near the end of their egg-laying period. This is an area of bare skin on the belly through which body heat passes readily to incubate the developing eggs. For additional heating action, extra blood vessels grow close to the exposed skin surface of the brood patch. Usually, the feathers in the patch area are shed automatically, but ducks and geese pluck their patch and use the plucked down to make an insulating nest lining.

True or False?
Birds can see color.

Killdeer

The Killdeer calls out its own name and, as with many other birds, that is how it got its common name to begin with. Like many ground-nesting birds, the young are precocial (pree-koh-shul) meaning that when they hatch they are fully feathered. Precocial young leave the nest very soon after hatching and do not return.

Bird Bills and Feet

The bills and feet of birds have to do the work that many other backboned animals do with their forelimbs. (Birds use their forelimbs almost exclusively for flying.)

Bills

Bills (or beaks) are mainly used for obtaining and grasping food, and sometimes also for processing it before swallowing. But bills also serve to preen, build nests, dig, turn eggs, fight and climb. Hence, depending on a particular bird's way of life, bill size and shape vary greatly.

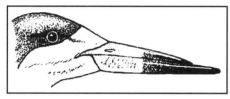

Black Skimmer
As the bird flies low with mouth open, the longer lower jaw slices through the water in search of fish.

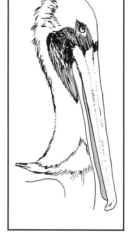

Painted Bunting
The short stout bill is designed to crack and husk seeds.

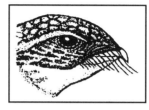

Brown Pelican
The huge pouch on the lower jaw is used to capture fish.

Chuck-will's-widow
The wide gaping bristle-fringed mouth sweeps in insects during flight.

Ruby-throated Hummingbird
The long thin bill is just right for inserting into flowers to get to the nectar.

Mallard (Duck)
The edges of the bill act like a sieve to sort out seeds and insects from the water.

Hummingbird

Feet

Birds use their feet for walking, grasping, climbing, perching, digging, scratching and swimming. Bird feet, like bird bills, are related to the life-styles of the birds.

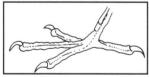

American Robin
A typical "perching" foot. The three toes in front and the rearward-facing toe curl themselves around branches. (More than half of the 9,300 species of birds are passerines or "perching birds.")

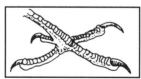

Golden-fronted Woodpecker
Two toes forward and two toes back give this foot a powerful grip for clinging to tree trunks.

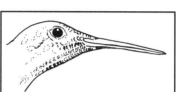

Perching muscles

Belted Kingfisher
The fused middle toes help in digging out nest tunnels in river banks.

Harris's Hawk
The powerful toes and strong, highly curved claws (called talons) help grasp prey.

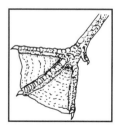

Mallard (Duck)
The webbing between the toes works like a paddle while swimming.

Wild Turkey
Like in all game birds, the foot is flat with a reduced backward-pointing toe. This is a real "walking" foot.

Spur (only on male)

Turkey footprint

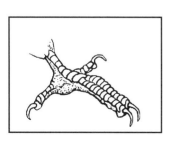

Field Notes for the Greater Roadrunner

Range   Nesting Place   Nest Type   Favorite Food

Size: Length 22", Wingspan 22"

Above: olive with white feather edgings
Below: buff streaked with brown
Crest: dark brown
Tail: extremely long, graduated with white tips, held cocked
Skin behind eyes (male): white in the front, pink in the back
Skin behind eyes (female): blue in the front, blue in the back
Voice is a descending series of soft, low "coo"s, not a "beep,
   beep, beep" like in the cartoon.

This Roadrunner has caught
a lizard. Reptiles are a
common source of food.

Greater Roadrunner

Full-sized
track

This bird is a cuckoo that lives on the ground and runs more than it flies. It has a long, black tail and the body is heavily streaked with brown and white. It has an obvious bushy crest. Look for it speeding across the ground on its long, strong legs. It builds a neat saucer-shaped nest usually among the thorns of a cactus plant and lays 3 to 6 white eggs. It hunts grasshoppers, lizards, snakes and rodents, quickly killing its prey with its strong pointed bill.

Field Notes for the Red-tailed Hawk

Range   Nesting Place   Nest Type   Favorite Food

Size: Length 18", Wingspan 48"

Plumage: mottled brown & white
Eye color: yellow to reddish brown
Belly band: dark
Primaries (wing tips): always black
Tail: reddish above, light pink beneath

— Did You Know That . . . —

Small birds, such as House Sparrows, sometimes build their tiny woven nests on the same large stick platforms that hawks and other raptors use for their own nesting purposes. The little birds are probably useful to their raptor "hosts" because they sound the alarm when an intruder gets too close. Maybe that's why they never seem to end up on their fierce neighbor's dinner menu!

True or False?
Birds are warm blooded.

Red-tailed Hawk

The Red-tailed Hawk is the most common hawk in Texas. It is one of a large group of hawks called buteos (beaut-ay-ohs). Unlike other hawks, buteos have broad, rounded wings and can often be seen soaring for long periods of time.

Field Notes for the Belted Kingfisher

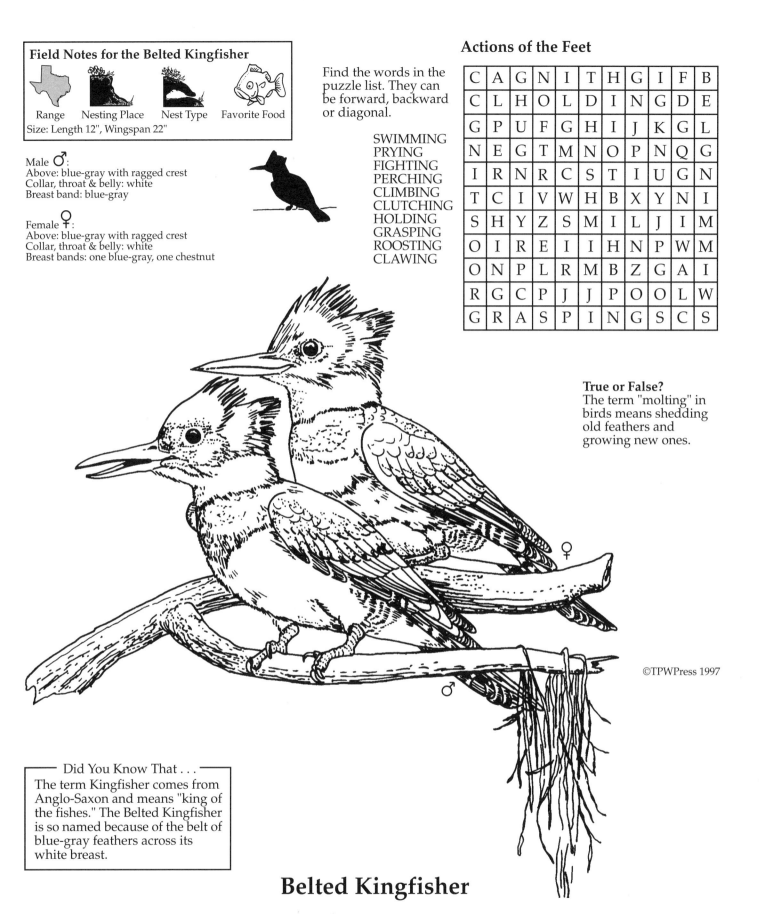

Range   Nesting Place   Nest Type   Favorite Food
Size: Length 12", Wingspan 22"

Male ♂:
Above: blue-gray with ragged crest
Collar, throat & belly: white
Breast band: blue-gray

Female ♀:
Above: blue-gray with ragged crest
Collar, throat & belly: white
Breast bands: one blue-gray, one chestnut

Actions of the Feet

Find the words in the puzzle list. They can be forward, backward or diagonal.

SWIMMING
PRYING
FIGHTING
PERCHING
CLIMBING
CLUTCHING
HOLDING
GRASPING
ROOSTING
CLAWING

C	A	G	N	I	T	H	G	I	F	B
C	L	H	O	L	D	I	N	G	D	E
G	P	U	F	G	H	I	J	K	G	L
N	E	G	T	M	N	O	P	N	Q	G
I	R	N	R	C	S	T	I	U	G	N
T	C	I	V	W	H	B	X	Y	N	I
S	H	Y	Z	S	M	I	L	J	I	M
O	I	R	E	I	I	H	N	P	W	M
O	N	P	L	R	M	B	Z	G	A	I
R	G	C	P	J	J	P	O	O	L	W
G	R	A	S	P	I	N	G	S	C	S

True or False?
The term "molting" in birds means shedding old feathers and growing new ones.

♀

©TPWPress 1997

♂

Did You Know That . . .
The term Kingfisher comes from Anglo-Saxon and means "king of the fishes." The Belted Kingfisher is so named because of the belt of blue-gray feathers across its white breast.

Belted Kingfisher

Texas has three species of kingfishers. The Belted Kingfisher is the most widespread of the three. Kingfishers, as their name suggests, feed on fish. They hunt by sitting up in a tree and looking for fish in the water. Hence, they need clear water to be successful. Once they have spotted the right-sized fish, they dive into the water to catch it.

13

Field Notes for the Scissor-tailed Flycatcher

Range   Nesting Place   Nest Type   Favorite Food
Size: Length 14", Wingspan 14"

Head, back & breast: pearl gray
Belly & wing lining: grayish washed with rose
Wings: black

©TPWPress 1997

Box Puzzle

Each of the letter boxes throughout the book contains an 8-letter word. It can be found by starting at one of the letters and reading either **clockwise** or **counter-clockwise**. In the example below the word SWALLOWS is found by starting at the **S** in the lower left corner and reading clockwise.

A	L	L
W		O
S	S	W

Example

A	L	L
W		O
S	S	W

SWALLOWS

Box 1

L	L	I
D		K
E	E	R

Name the bird in box 1.

_____

Scissor-tailed Flycatcher

The Scissor-tailed Flycatcher can easily be recognized by its long tail. The tail of an adult male is almost twice as long as its body; the female's is somewhat shorter. In the U.S., this flycatcher is found only in Texas and Oklahoma. As its name suggests, this bird feeds mostly on insects which it often catches on the wing.

Did You Know That . . .

Many birds swallow sand, grit or pebbles to
help them grind up their food. The swallowed
materials are stored in a muscular section of
the stomach called the gizzard. This organ is
lined with bony ridges, and it is here that
grains, acorns, nuts, beetles, snails and other
hard-shelled food items are rapidly tossed
about and crushed. Thus, in birds – none of
which have teeth – the gizzard with its stony
materials can be said to take the place of the
chewing and crushing teeth found in many
other animals.

U	L	B
E		D
B	I	R

Box 2

Name the bird in box 2.

_____

Find the words in the
puzzle list. They can be
forward or backward or
diagonal. Make a list of
the remaining letters
and put them together
in a sentence.

GRASPING
CARRYING
SCRATCHING
DIGGING
CRACKING
CATCHING
EATING
CUTTING
HATCHING
CLIMBING
EGG TURNING

Actions of the Bill

G	N	I	H	C	T	A	R	C	S	I
F	C	L	I	M	B	I	N	G	G	Y
G	D	I	G	G	I	N	G	N	O	U
N	S	G	R	A	S	P	I	N	G	G
I	E	E	A	F	E	N	E	D	I	N
H	N	C	A	R	R	Y	I	N	G	I
C	G	B	I	U	R	D	N	O	N	H
T	C	U	T	T	I	N	G	T	I	C
A	I	G	C	E	I	T	S	B	T	T
C	G	E	H	A	V	I	O	R	A	A
E	C	R	A	C	K	I	N	G	E	H

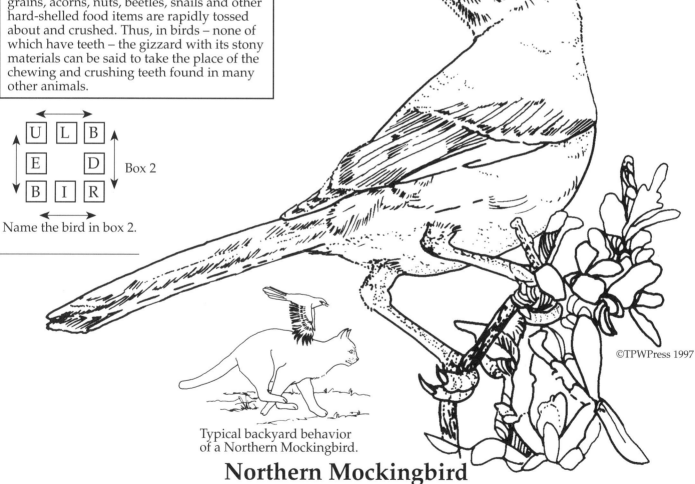

©TPWPress 1997

Typical backyard behavior
of a Northern Mockingbird.

Northern Mockingbird

The Northern Mockingbird is the state bird of Texas. It belongs in a family of birds called thrashers.
Many of the birds in that family are mimics, but none can match the Northern Mockingbird which
imitates the songs of other birds, and occassionally other sounds. Mockingbirds can be recognized by
the large white patches on their wings and tail.

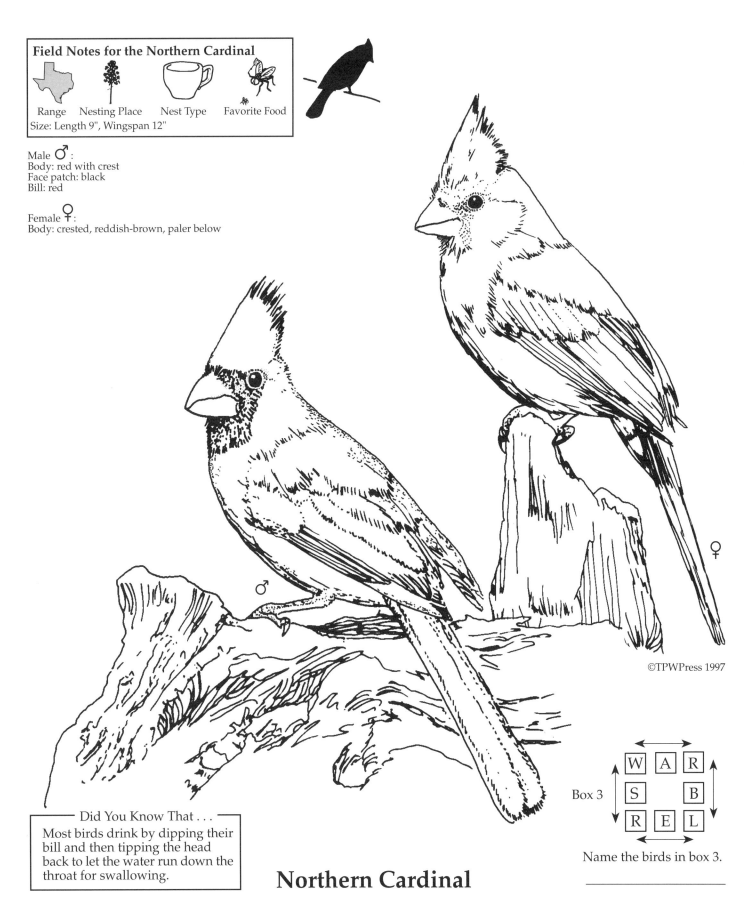

Field Notes for the Northern Cardinal

Range | Nesting Place | Nest Type | Favorite Food

Size: Length 9", Wingspan 12"

Male ♂ :
Body: red with crest
Face patch: black
Bill: red

Female ♀ :
Body: crested, reddish-brown, paler below

©TPWPress 1997

— Did You Know That . . . —
Most birds drink by dipping their
bill and then tipping the head
back to let the water run down the
throat for swallowing.

Box 3

W	A	R
S		B
R	E	L

Name the birds in box 3.

Northern Cardinal

The bright red plumage of the male Northern Cardinal is well known throughout the eastern United States. The female is mostly brown, tinged with red on the wings, crest and tail. Seven states in the eastern U.S. count the Northern Cardinal as their state bird. Cardinals are named after officials in the Roman Catholic Church, called cardinals, who wear red robes.

Field Notes for the Painted Bunting

Range   Nesting Place   Nest Type   Favorite Food

Size: Length 6", Wingspan 9"

Male ♂:
Head: blue-violet
Underparts and rump: red
Back: green
Wings & tail: dark red

Female ♀:
Above: bright yellow-green
Below: paler yellow-green

— Did You Know That . . . —
Some of the smaller birds, like warblers and sparrows, sip on dewdrops for their water needs.

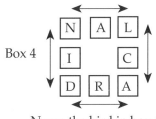

Box 4

N	A	L
I		C
D	R	A

Name the bird in box 4.

_____

©TPWPress 1997

Color the Painted Bunting making sure to label your illustration male or female.

— Did You Know That . . . —
Female and male birds of the same species often look different. The male is usually the more colorful bird since he uses his colors to "show off" for the female and to "warn off" other males. The dull colors of the female help to camouflage her on the nest.

True or False?
Feathers evolved from the scales of the reptile ancestors of birds.

Painted Bunting

The male Painted Bunting is one of the most colorful birds in Texas. The bright plumage is not attained by young males until they are two years old. This is unusual among songbirds. The one-year-old males are solid green like the females, but they do sing and defend territories.

17

Field Notes for the Mourning Dove

Range	Nesting Place	Nest Type	Favorite Food

Size: Length 12", Wingspan 18"

Above: tan
Cap: gray
Bill: brown
Whisker: black
Eye ring: blue
Eyes: brown
Side of neck: purplish-bronze highlights
Wings: brownish with spots of dark brown
Below: tan-buff
Feet: pink
Tail: edged in white

What's an "egg tooth"?

We all know that modern birds don't have teeth. What then is the "egg tooth," which all birds have when they hatch? It is a temporary toothlike structure at the end of the upper beak that helps the chick get out of what would otherwise become its tomb — namely, the tough egg shell that has protected its development as an embryo.

Here is how it works. When the chick is ready to hatch, it swallows most of the liquid inside the egg, draws the remaining yolk into its lower body, and pushes its head into an air space that has now opened up next to the shell. There, it begins to breathe air and peep. Then, by contracting powerful muscles along the back of its head and neck, it drives the egg tooth into the shell, making a small hole. Finally, further movements of the head and feet crack the shell enough for the chick to come out. After hatching, the egg tooth drops off.

Did You Know That . . .

Doves and pigeons drink by dipping their bill and then sucking up the water. (That's unlike most other birds.)

Can you identify these perched birds?

Mourning Dove

Mourning Doves get their name from the mournful cooing sounds these birds make. Mourning Doves nest three or four times during the breeding season. They begin nesting as early as February in South Texas.

Build a Simple Feeder

A square, gallon-sized plastic milk jug can be converted into a simple feeder quite easily. It may not be as attractive as a commercial feeder, but the birds won't mind.

Mark the jug.

Items you will need:
1 square, gallon-sized plastic milk jug
2 wooden dowels,
    each ½ inch round and 10 inches long
a marking pen
a ruler
a pair of scissors
some wild bird seed
and a creative method of mounting the
    bird feeder to a post, tree or the house.

Cut the openings.

Mark for the openings
The openings should be about 2½ inches from the bottom of the jug, 3 inches wide and 4 inches high, on the two sides opposite the handle.

Cut the openings
Arching the tops of these openings will make them more decorative. (A hobby knife is a good tool for this job, but because these knives usually are very sharp, it would be wise to get help from an adult.)

Add perches.

Add perches to the milk-jug feeder
Drill a set of holes through the jug about ¼ inch below one of the openings. (Use the point of the scissors to start the hole.) Insert a ½ inch round wooden dowel, cut to a length of 10 inches, through these holes. Drill another set of holes through the jug ½ inch below the other opening and insert a second dowel. The ends should extend about 2 inches beyond the sides with the openings to form perches. Drilling one set of holes lower than the other set allows the dowels to cross inside the jug.

Your birdfeeder is ready to use. You could tie it outside or attach the milk jug feeder to a piece of wood with a couple of wood screws through the handle. Mount the pieces of wood on a post, tree or any structure in view from your window.

Completed bird feeder with wild bird seed.

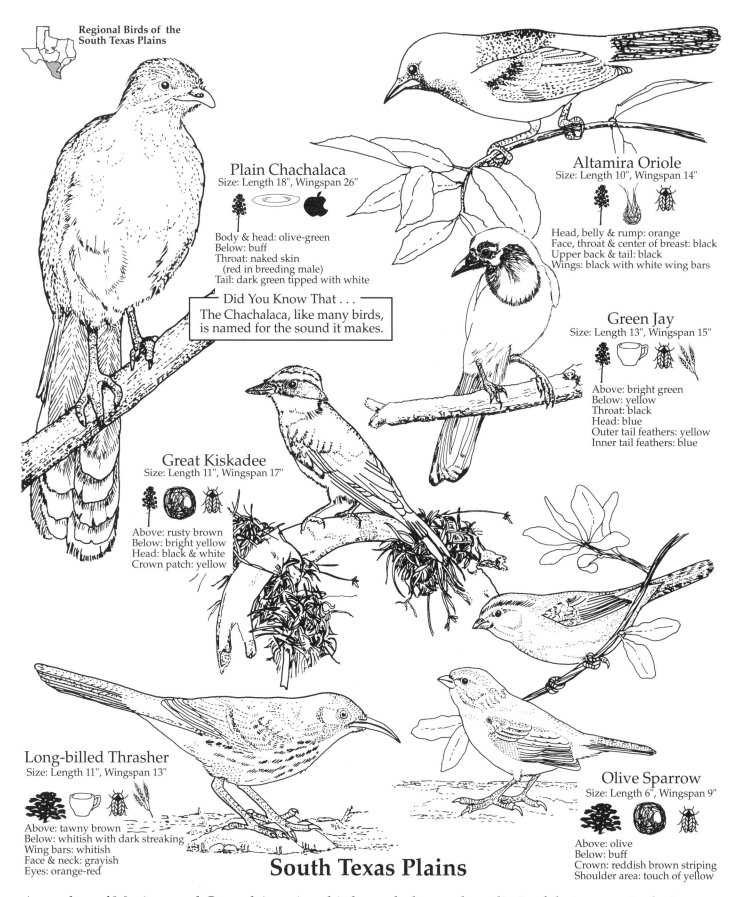

Plain Chachalaca
Size: Length 18", Wingspan 26"

Body & head: olive-green
Below: buff
Throat: naked skin
  (red in breeding male)
Tail: dark green tipped with white

Did You Know That . . .
The Chachalaca, like many birds,
is named for the sound it makes.

Altamira Oriole
Size: Length 10", Wingspan 14"

Head, belly & rump: orange
Face, throat & center of breast: black
Upper back & tail: black
Wings: black with white wing bars

Green Jay
Size: Length 13", Wingspan 15"

Above: bright green
Below: yellow
Throat: black
Head: blue
Outer tail feathers: yellow
Inner tail feathers: blue

Great Kiskadee
Size: Length 11", Wingspan 17"

Above: rusty brown
Below: bright yellow
Head: black & white
Crown patch: yellow

Long-billed Thrasher
Size: Length 11", Wingspan 13"

Above: tawny brown
Below: whitish with dark streaking
Wing bars: whitish
Face & neck: grayish
Eyes: orange-red

Olive Sparrow
Size: Length 6", Wingspan 9"

Above: olive
Below: buff
Crown: reddish brown striping
Shoulder area: touch of yellow

South Texas Plains

A number of Mexican and Central American birds reach the northern limit of their range in the Lower Rio Grande Valley of Texas. This part of Texas has a subtropical climate, meaning that it's close to being tropical. Thousands of people make trips to this part of Texas to see these special birds found nowhere else in the United States.

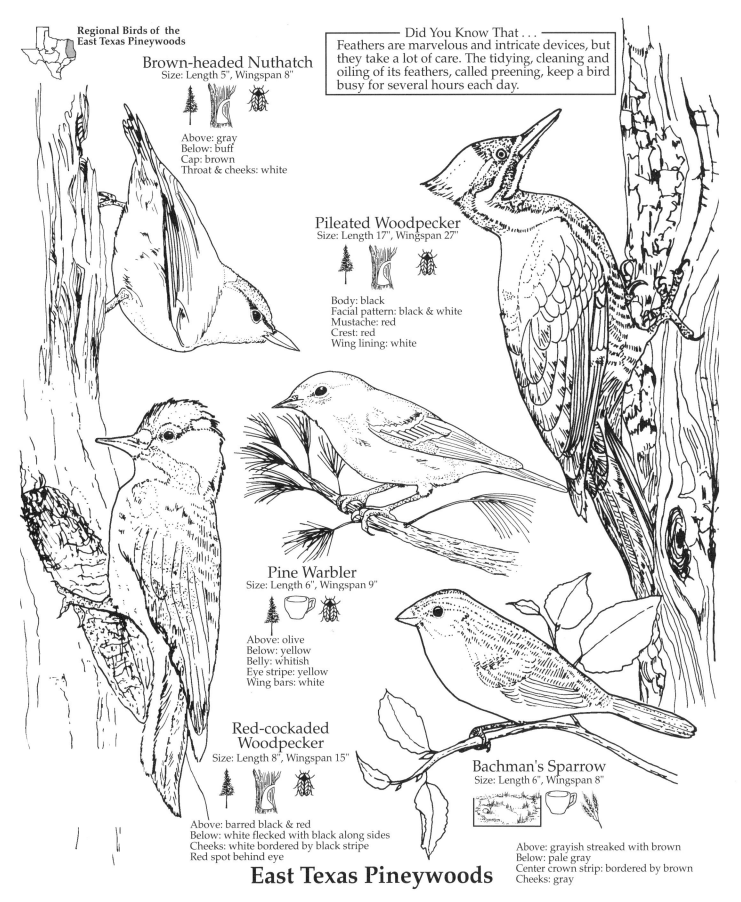

Regional Birds of the East Texas Pineywoods

Brown-headed Nuthatch
Size: Length 5", Wingspan 8"

Above: gray
Below: buff
Cap: brown
Throat & cheeks: white

Pileated Woodpecker
Size: Length 17", Wingspan 27"

Body: black
Facial pattern: black & white
Mustache: red
Crest: red
Wing lining: white

Pine Warbler
Size: Length 6", Wingspan 9"

Above: olive
Below: yellow
Belly: whitish
Eye stripe: yellow
Wing bars: white

Red-cockaded Woodpecker
Size: Length 8", Wingspan 15"

Above: barred black & red
Below: white flecked with black along sides
Cheeks: white bordered by black stripe
Red spot behind eye

Bachman's Sparrow
Size: Length 6", Wingspan 8"

Above: grayish streaked with brown
Below: pale gray
Center crown strip: bordered by brown
Cheeks: gray

East Texas Pineywoods

The pine forests of East Texas provide habitat for a group of birds found nowhere else in Texas. Many of these species are endemic to the southeastern United States. When a species is called endemic to an area, it means that it is found only in that place. (The Pileated Woodpecker can be found in other habitats and can be seen away from the pineywoods of East Texas.)

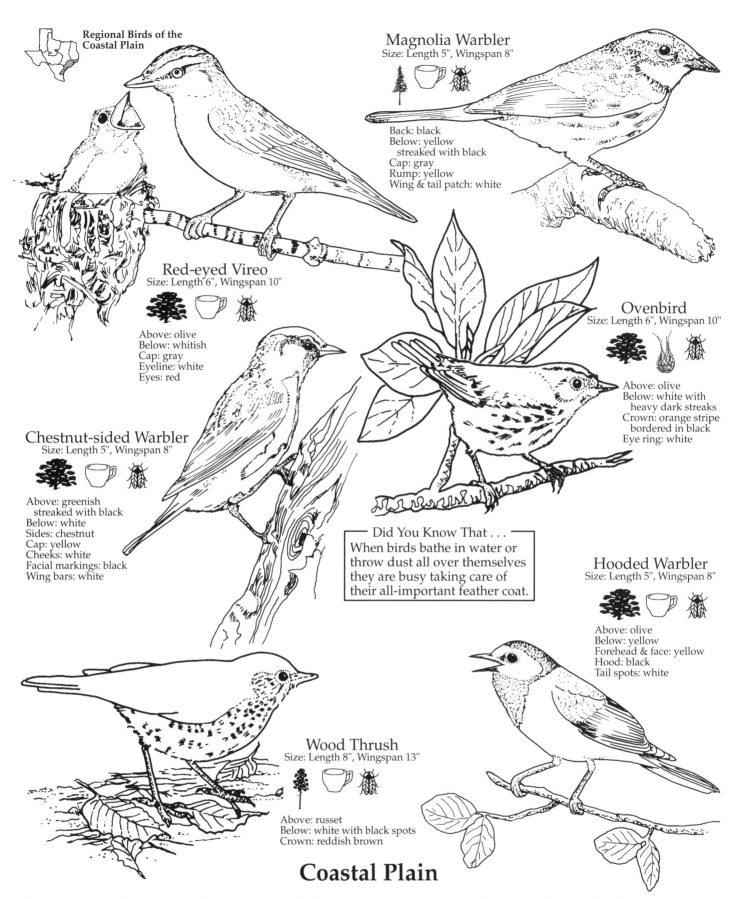

Regional Birds of the Coastal Plain

Magnolia Warbler
Size: Length 5", Wingspan 8"

Back: black
Below: yellow
    streaked with black
Cap: gray
Rump: yellow
Wing & tail patch: white

Red-eyed Vireo
Size: Length 6", Wingspan 10"

Above: olive
Below: whitish
Cap: gray
Eyeline: white
Eyes: red

Ovenbird
Size: Length 6", Wingspan 10"

Above: olive
Below: white with
    heavy dark streaks
Crown: orange stripe
    bordered in black
Eye ring: white

Chestnut-sided Warbler
Size: Length 5", Wingspan 8"

Above: greenish
    streaked with black
Below: white
Sides: chestnut
Cap: yellow
Cheeks: white
Facial markings: black
Wing bars: white

┌─ Did You Know That . . . ─┐
When birds bathe in water or
throw dust all over themselves
they are busy taking care of
their all-important feather coat.
└───────────────────────────┘

Hooded Warbler
Size: Length 5", Wingspan 8"

Above: olive
Below: yellow
Forehead & face: yellow
Hood: black
Tail spots: white

Wood Thrush
Size: Length 8", Wingspan 13"

Above: russet
Below: white with black spots
Crown: reddish brown

Coastal Plain

Spring migration on the Texas coast, and the upper coast in particular, is a place to find many species of neotropical migrants. Neotropical means "new tropics" and neotropical migrants are birds that migrate to Central or South America from North America each fall. These birds then fly north again in the spring.

Did You Know That . . .
Songbirds shake themselves to throw off water by vibrating their wings and tail and ruffling their feathers.

Green Kingfisher
Size: Length 9", Wingspan 12"

Male ♂:
Above: green
Collar & belly: white
Breast band: chestnut

Female ♀:
Above: green
Collar & belly: white
Breast band: greenish

Lesser Goldfinch
Size: Length 5", Wingspan 8"

Above: black
Below: yellow
Primaries patches: white

Vermilion Flycatcher
Size: Length 8", Wingspan 15"

Male ♂:
Above: black
Below: scarlet
Cap: scarlet

Female ♀:
Above: brownish
Eyebrow: white
Breast: white faintly
  streaked with brown
Throat: white
Belly: orangish or yellowish

Black-capped Vireo
Size: Length 5", Wingspan 7"

Above: grayish-green
Below: white
Head: black with white spectacles

Golden-cheeked Warbler
Size: Length 5", Wingspan 8"

Above: black
Bib: black
Belly: white
Cheeks: golden
Eye line: black

Edwards Plateau (Hill Country)

The Edwards Plateau or Hill Country is in the center of the state. As a result, its birdlife is a mixture of eastern and western species. The oak-juniper woodlands of the plateau provide habitat for one of its most distinctive species, the Golden-cheeked Warbler. This warbler is the only bird whose nesting range is entirely in Texas. It spends the winter in Central America.

Winter Feeding Station

A well-equipped winter-feeding station should have a feeder of some type for seeds, a container for suet or bird-seed cake mixtures and a water source.

Make a Pine-Cone Feeder.

Select a large pine cone. Screw an eye-screw into the stem of the pine cone. Cover the pine cone with peanut butter and roll it in bird seed. Tie one end of a piece of string to the eye-screw and the other end to a branch. Don't feed wild birds the bird seed sold for cage birds because that mixture does not contain the right kinds of seeds. You can purchase "Wild Bird Seed" or "Chick Scratch" and be sure that it contains grit. Among the seeds that birds like are sunflower, millet and hemp seeds as well as cracked corn.

Golden-fronted Woodpecker at suet feeding station.

Make a Suet Cake.

Melt 2 ounces of lard in a pan. Ask an adult to help. Stir in 2 ounces of wild bird seed. Pour the mixture into a plastic container. Leave the cake to cool and harden. Place the cooled cake in a plastic strawberry container. Tie the cake to a branch.

Suet is primarily a cold-weather food. In warm weather it can melt and stick to a bird's feathers, causing loss of insulation and ability to fly and possibly even loss of feathers.

Make Peanut Chains.

Purchase some raw peanuts in their shells. Tie the peanuts into a row with a string around their middles. Tie about 10 to 12 nuts on each string and hang them up from a branch or the edge of a feeding station.

Be Bird Friendly! Make a Bird Warning for your Window.

Migrating birds that are just passing through can be confused by large windows. They may try to fly through them and stun themselves. You can help by hanging a warning in your window. A hawk shape works well because most birds will keep away from hawks.

Enlarge the hawk shape given here onto a piece of black poster board. Carefully cut out around the edges. Wrap in plastic to protect it from the rain. Attach a string to the head of the hawk cutout, and thumbtack the other end of the string to the top of your window frame. It will move about in the wind and look more realistic.

Be a real Cut-up!

Innocent-looking plastic six-pack yokes can be death traps for birds that become tangled in them.

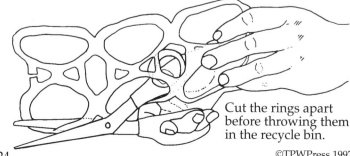

Cut the rings apart before throwing them in the recycle bin.

24

©TPWPress 1997

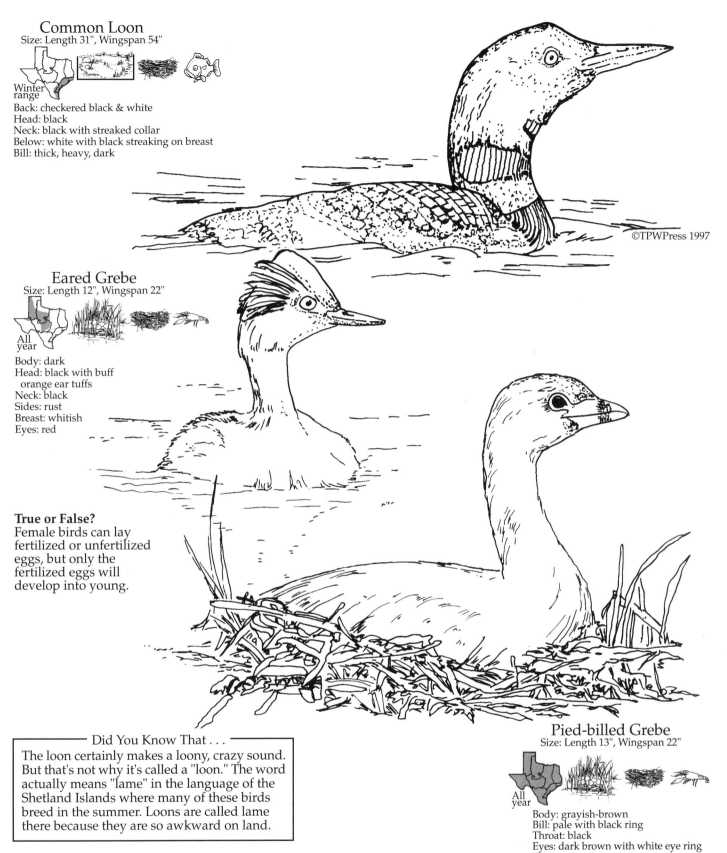

Common Loon
Size: Length 31", Wingspan 54"

Winter range

Back: checkered black & white
Head: black
Neck: black with streaked collar
Below: white with black streaking on breast
Bill: thick, heavy, dark

©TPWPress 1997

Eared Grebe
Size: Length 12", Wingspan 22"

All year

Body: dark
Head: black with buff
  orange ear tufts
Neck: black
Sides: rust
Breast: whitish
Eyes: red

True or False?
Female birds can lay fertilized or unfertilized eggs, but only the fertilized eggs will develop into young.

┌─── Did You Know That . . . ───┐
The loon certainly makes a loony, crazy sound.
But that's not why it's called a "loon." The word
actually means "lame" in the language of the
Shetland Islands where many of these birds
breed in the summer. Loons are called lame
there because they are so awkward on land.
└─────────────────────────────┘

Pied-billed Grebe
Size: Length 13", Wingspan 22"

All year

Body: grayish-brown
Bill: pale with black ring
Throat: black
Eyes: dark brown with white eye ring

Loons and Grebes

The Common Loon is the only loon that is common in Texas. Loons feed on fish and they are tremendous divers. Unlike most other birds, loons have solid, not hollow, bones. This permits them to go underwater easily. The Pied-billed and Eared Grebes are the only grebes that regularly nest in Texas, occurring in greater numbers in the state during the winter. Unlike loons, grebes feed primarily on aquatic insects.

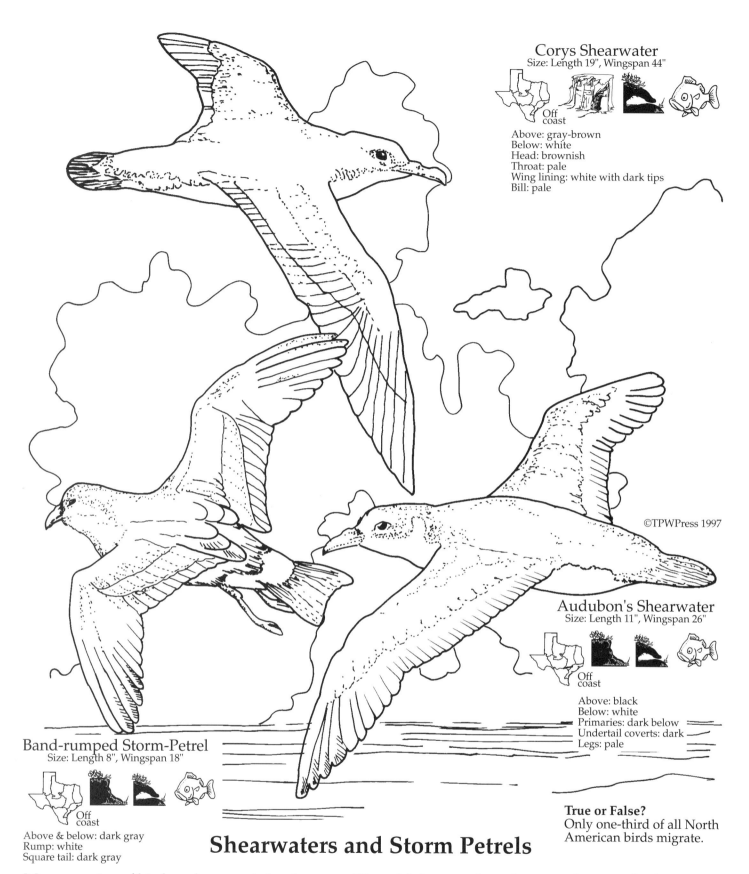

Corys Shearwater
Size: Length 19", Wingspan 44"

Off coast

Above: gray-brown
Below: white
Head: brownish
Throat: pale
Wing lining: white with dark tips
Bill: pale

©TPWPress 1997

Audubon's Shearwater
Size: Length 11", Wingspan 26"

Off coast

Above: black
Below: white
Primaries: dark below
Undertail coverts: dark
Legs: pale

Band-rumped Storm-Petrel
Size: Length 8", Wingspan 18"

Off coast

Above & below: dark gray
Rump: white
Square tail: dark gray

True or False?
Only one-third of all North American birds migrate.

Shearwaters and Storm Petrels

Many species of birds only come to land to nest. These birds are referred to as pelagics, which means living on the open ocean. They have many adaptations that allow them to survive. They have long narrow wings that permit them to glide for long periods. Their nostrils are encased in tubes on top of the bill. Special glands near the nostrils help get rid of excess salt in these seabirds' bloodstream. The glands work like kidneys and pump out salt through the tubes. Only a few pelagic species can be found in Texas waters.

Snow Goose
Size: Length 28", Wingspan 57"

Winter range

Body: white
Primaries: black
Bill: red
Legs: red

Canada Goose
Size: Length 26 to 48", Wingspan 54 to 84"

Winter range

Body: grayish-brown above,
   grayish below
Head: black with white
   chin strap
Neck: black
Belly, rump & undertail: white
Tail: black

Greater White-fronted Goose
Size: Length 28", Wingspan 57"

Winter range

Body: brown barred with buff on back
Breast & upper belly: speckled with black
Lowerbelly & undertail: white
Bill: pinkish with white feathers at base, edged in black
Legs: orange

©TPWPress 1997

Geese

Thousands of Canada, Greater White-fronted and Snow Geese migrate from their summer breeding grounds in Canada to the Texas coast. Snow Geese have two color phases or forms: white and gray. The gray phase is commonly called Blue Goose. Almost all of the world's population of Blue Geese winter in Texas.

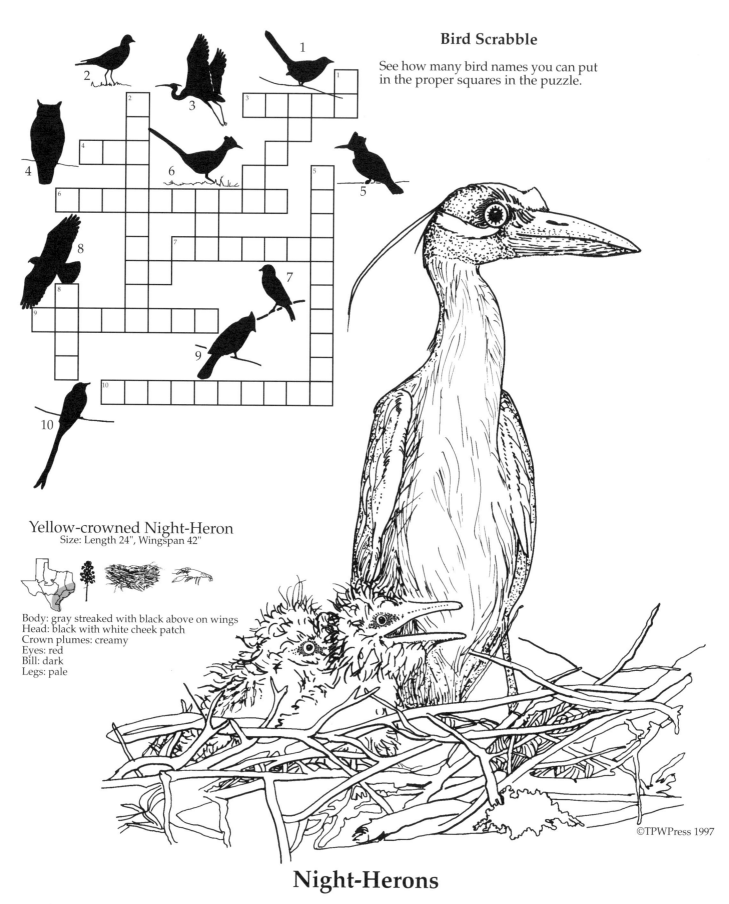

Bird Scrabble

See how many bird names you can put in the proper squares in the puzzle.

Yellow-crowned Night-Heron
Size: Length 24", Wingspan 42"

Body: gray streaked with black above on wings
Head: black with white cheek patch
Crown plumes: creamy
Eyes: red
Bill: dark
Legs: pale

©TPWPress 1997

Night-Herons

As the name suggests, night-herons are mainly nocturnal. There are two species in Texas: the Black-crowned Night-Heron and the Yellow-crowned Night-Heron. Like other herons, the Black-crowned Night-Heron feeds mainly on fish and frogs, but the Yellow-crowned Night-Heron seems to prefer crayfish and crabs.

Harris's Hawk
Size: Length 21", Wingspan 45"

All year

Body: dark brown
Shoulders & thighs: chestnut
Legs: yellow
Tail: dark with broad white band at
    base & narrow white terminal strip
Eyes: brown
Wing lining: chestnut

─── Did You Know That . . . ───
Hawk comes from the same Anglo-Saxon
root as "have" (in the sense of "grasp").

When falconry, the sport of hunting with
falcons, was popular, "merlin" was the name
used for a female falcon. Falcon itself comes
from the Latin *falx* ("sickle"), for the bird's
sickle-like talons and beak.

Peregrine means "wanderer" from the same
Latin root as "peregrinate" and pilgrim.

Peregrine Falcon
Size: Length 18", Wingspan 40"

Winter range

Above: dark gray
Below: white with spotting & barring on belly & thighs
Crown: black
Cheeks: black with white neck patch
Eyes: brown
Eye ring: yellow
Legs: yellow

Birds of Prey

Among Texas' birds of prey are the Harris's Hawk and the Peregrine Falcon. The Harris's Hawk is a very social bird, its young of the year remaining with the parents throughout the winter. Family groups of four or five birds are not uncommon. Peregrine Falcons often catch their prey in the air by diving at them from above. These dives have been estimated at up to 180 miles per hour.

Make A Bird Blind.

Now that you have installed your bird feeding station, you find that every time you try to watch a bird, if you move even a little to get a better view, the bird flies away when it sees you. What you need now is a bird blind. That way, you can get a better look at the birds that live in or pass through your own back-yard. Be sure to keep notes about what you see. If you have a tape recorder, you might even want to record some of the sounds the birds make.

Items you will need:

Large box, with holes to look through
Books to help identify the birds you see
Binoculars
Your bird journal or a notebook
Tape recorder

The most important things you need for birdwatching are patience and quiet. Your own eyes and ears are your most important equipment.

Stay quietly in one place and you will see more birds than if you move around noisily. Birds can be found almost anywhere there is food, water and shelter.

You'll see different birds at different times of the year. Birds' activities change with the seasons, too.

Birds are most active in the early morning and early evening. They eat a lot then, before and after their night's rest.

Birds choose their nesting places very carefully.

Please watch nesting birds only from a distance. Don't scare them by moving tree branches or grass for a better view. Never touch nests, eggs or birds on a nest.

Use binoculars if you want to get a better and closer view of the birds.

Study each bird you see. Notice its feathers. Watch how it moves. Listen to its call and songs.

Field guides can help you identify birds. Keep a field guide with you in the blind.

Bird Guides
Tape recorder
TORI"S Journal

Keep A Journal.

Use a pencil – it's easier to sketch, and won't run if your journal gets wet.

May 3, 1997   The field behind Melissa's house
10:19 a.m.
Blue Jay
-have been observing & trying to photograph for approx. 45 minutes.
-has been singing very frequently during entire

May 10, 1997   McKinney Falls State Park
8:30 a.m.
I saw a painted bunting while we were at the park

May 12, 1997   School ball field, near the back fence
12:00 a.m.
-Most of the birds are brown but I saw one Cardinal and a Blue jay squawking at each other

June 20, 1997   The Zoo
10:30 a.m.
Greater Flamingo
-have been observing for approx. 5 minutes.
-no singing or noise was made during entire observation.
-It was taller than I thought it would be.
-swished bill through the water to get drink or food

-Pink bird with heavy, right-angled bill, pink, with black on the edge
-long legs with webbed toes
-long neck
-black primaries

Black

Remember, birds like it quiet.

30

Scaled Quail
Size: Length 11", Wingspan 15"

Above: grayish-brown
Neck & nape: scaled gray & black
Head: brown with erect brown crest tipped with buff
Flanks & belly: spotted & scalloped brown & buff

Gambel's Quail
Size: Length 11", Wingspan 15"

Above & upper breast: pale gray
Nape: streaked with black
Cap: chestnut with long, black, curling topknot
Face & throat: black
Lower breast & belly: beige with black central spot
Flanks: chestnut spotted with white

Northern Bobwhite
Size: Length 10", Wingspan 15"

Above: brown & gray mottled with dark brown & white
Sides: chestnut spotted with white
Breast & belly: white scalloped with black
Crown: chestnut with short ragged crest
Eyebrow & throat: white

Montezuma Quail
Size: Length 9", Wingspan 17"

Bulbs

Back: chestnut & brown with white streaking
Facial pattern: black & white (like a hockey goalie mask)
Chest: chestnut
Breast & belly: chestnut, spotted with white on both sides
Wings: brown, spotted with dark brown

Lesser Prairie-Chicken
Size: Length 16", Wingspan 26"

Above: mottled brown & white
Below: barred tan & white
Throat sacks: reddish-orange
Tail: dark

Attwater's Greater Prairie-Chicken
Size: Length 18", Wingspan 28"

Above: mottled brown & white
Below: barred tan & white
Throat sacks: golden
Tail: dark

©TPWPress 1997

Quail and Grouse

Texas is home to four species of quail and two species of grouse. The grouse are the Greater and Lesser Prairie-Chickens and they are very similar. The Texas subspecies of the Greater Prairie-Chicken is called the Attwater's Greater Prairie-Chicken. It is very rare and found in only a few places along the coastal prairies. The four kinds of quail are the Scaled Quail, Gambel's Quail, the Northern Bobwhite and the Montezuma Quail. The Northern Bobwhite gets its name from its call.

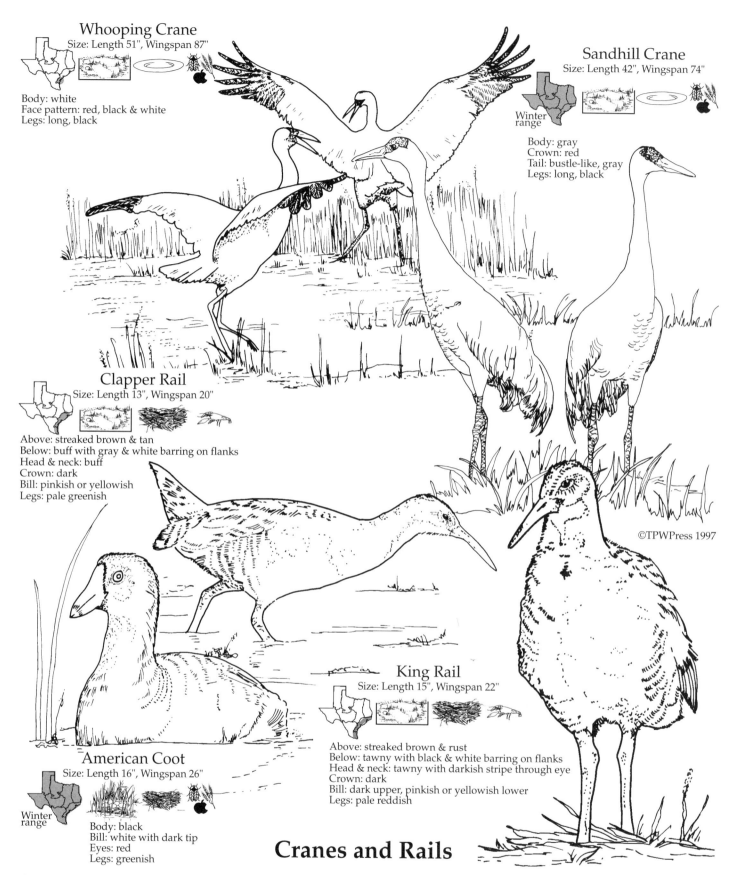

Whooping Crane
Size: Length 51", Wingspan 87"

Body: white
Face pattern: red, black & white
Legs: long, black

Sandhill Crane
Size: Length 42", Wingspan 74"

Winter range

Body: gray
Crown: red
Tail: bustle-like, gray
Legs: long, black

Clapper Rail
Size: Length 13", Wingspan 20"

Above: streaked brown & tan
Below: buff with gray & white barring on flanks
Head & neck: buff
Crown: dark
Bill: pinkish or yellowish
Legs: pale greenish

©TPWPress 1997

King Rail
Size: Length 15", Wingspan 22"

Above: streaked brown & rust
Below: tawny with black & white barring on flanks
Head & neck: tawny with darkish stripe through eye
Crown: dark
Bill: dark upper, pinkish or yellowish lower
Legs: pale reddish

American Coot
Size: Length 16", Wingspan 26"

Winter range

Body: black
Bill: white with dark tip
Eyes: red
Legs: greenish

Cranes and Rails

Cranes and rails are very closely related even though they look very different. Texas is the winter home to both of North America's cranes, the Whooping and Sandhill Cranes. The Whooping Crane is one of the world's rarest birds. Most rails are very shy and stay hidden in marshes. The Clapper and King Rails are almost identical, but Clappers are normally found in salt marshes while King Rails are usually in freshwater marshes. The American Coot is actually a rail and is very common throughout Texas.

American Oystercatcher
Size: Length 19", Wingspan 35"

Back: brown
Breast & belly: white
Hood: black
Bill: bright orange
Eye ring: red
Legs: pinkish

©TPWPress 1997

Laughing Gull
Size: Length 17", Wingspan 40"

Head: black
Back & wings: gray
Wing tips: black
Collar: white
Underparts & tail: white
Bill: scarlet
Legs: black

Ruddy Turnstone
Size: Length 10", Wingspan 19"

Above: reddish brown
Below: white
Breast: black
Face pattern: black & white
Wing stripes: white
Tail band: white
Legs: orange

Caspian Tern
Size: Length 21", Wingspan 52"

Underparts: white
Back & wings: light gray
Large bill: blood-orange
Cap: black
Face & neck: white

Birds of Gulf Beaches

Texas' coastal beaches and marshes are home to an amazing variety of birds. This is particularly true of shallow marshes and bays. However, there are many birds that are found primarily on beaches. Such birds often feed on fish and other animals that wash up on the beach. Gulls in particular are scavengers that will eat almost anything.

33

Field Sketches For Your Journal

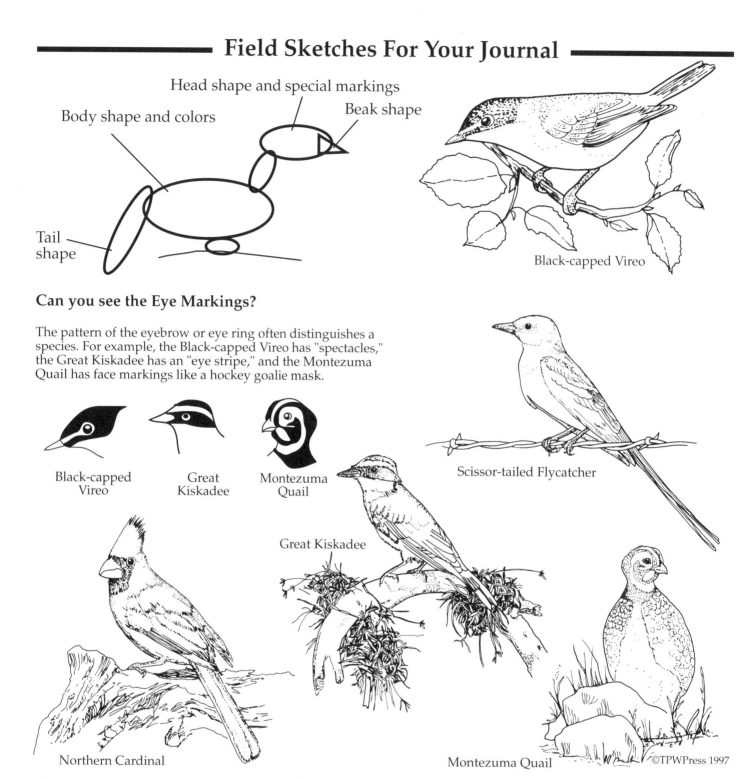

Head shape and special markings

Body shape and colors

Beak shape

Tail shape

Black-capped Vireo

Can you see the Eye Markings?

The pattern of the eyebrow or eye ring often distinguishes a species. For example, the Black-capped Vireo has "spectacles," the Great Kiskadee has an "eye stripe," and the Montezuma Quail has face markings like a hockey goalie mask.

Black-capped Vireo

Great Kiskadee

Montezuma Quail

Scissor-tailed Flycatcher

Great Kiskadee

Northern Cardinal

Montezuma Quail

©TPWPress 1997

When you see a bird you don't recognize, don't try to look it up in your bird guide right away. The bird will most likely fly off before you can find it in the guide. Instead, make a quick sketch in your journal with a pencil. You can make a good drawing of the main features by outlining the simple shapes shown above. Then add the most important details.

Where are the main patches of color?

What shape is the tail?

Can you see the shape of the beak?

Make a note of what the bird was doing and any information that will help you identify it. Now you can look it up in the bird guide. For each bird you see, write down the date you saw it and what kind of habitat it was in.

A car makes a very good blind. Be prepared to wait a while, the birds need to get used to the car; keep quiet and still inside.

Common Nighthawk
Size: Length 9", Wingspan 23"

Summer range

no nest

Above: mottled dark brown, gray & white
Below: whitish
Primaries band: white
Tail band: white

Barred Owl
Size: Length 18", Wingspan 42"

All year

Above: brown mottled with white
Throat & breast: white barred with brown
Belly: white streaked with brown
Eyes: dark

Eastern Screech-Owl
Size: Length 8", Wingspan 22"

All year

Eyes: yellow
Bill: pale
Red phase: Above reddish brown, streaked with rust
Below: brown & white
Facial disc: rust with white eyebrows
Gray phase: similar to red phase but gray
rather than rust

Owls and Nightjars

©TPWPress 1997

Owls and nightjars are both primarily night-time or nocturnal groups of birds. Most people readily recognize owls, but they are not as familiar with nightjars (which include the Whip-poor-will, Chuck-will's-widow, nighthawks and others). These birds feed on insects as they fly, so they have very large mouths to help them catch their food. They also have distinctive voices. Whip-poor-wills and Chuck-will's-widows are named after the song they sing. Most nightjars are nocturnal, with the exception of the nighthawks, which can be seen on summer evenings at dusk catching insects.

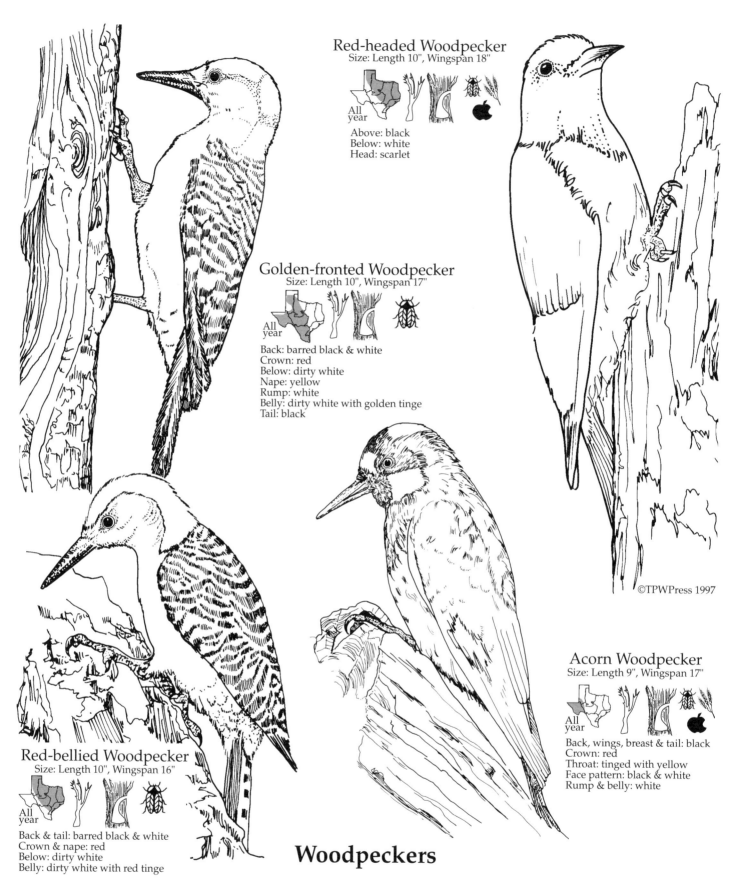

Red-headed Woodpecker
Size: Length 10", Wingspan 18"

All year

Above: black
Below: white
Head: scarlet

Golden-fronted Woodpecker
Size: Length 10", Wingspan 17"

All year

Back: barred black & white
Crown: red
Below: dirty white
Nape: yellow
Rump: white
Belly: dirty white with golden tinge
Tail: black

©TPWPress 1997

Acorn Woodpecker
Size: Length 9", Wingspan 17"

All year

Back, wings, breast & tail: black
Crown: red
Throat: tinged with yellow
Face pattern: black & white
Rump & belly: white

Red-bellied Woodpecker
Size: Length 10", Wingspan 16"

All year

Back & tail: barred black & white
Crown & nape: red
Below: dirty white
Belly: dirty white with red tinge

Woodpeckers

Woodpeckers have special adaptations that allow them to feed on wood-boring insects. They have powerful sharp bills with which they chisel out insect food and nest holes. Their extremely long, barbed tongues are used to extract insects from holes. All have sharp curved claws on their four toes, two of which point forward and two back, making for a strong grip while climbing. In addition, stiff tail feathers serve as props while moving along trees.

36

Eastern Kingbird
Size: Length 9", Wingspan 15"

Summer range

Above: black
Below: white
Wings: gray
Tail band: white at the tip
Red crest is usually not visible.

---— Did You Know That . . . ———
Kingbirds are probably named for their aggressive behavior, considered typical of kings and other rulers.

Box 5

S	H	E
A		R
R	H	T

Name the bird in box 5.

_____

Ash-throated Flycatcher
Size: Length 9", Wingspan 13"

Summer range

Above: brown
Throat & breast: grayish-white
Belly: pale yellow

©TPWPress 1997

Tyrant Flycatchers

Most of the group of birds called tyrant flycatchers have a large head and bristle-like feathers in the face area. Kingbirds, phoebes and most species of flycatchers belong in this group.

The Eastern Kingbird is common to many different habitats in the eastern half of the state. The Ash-throated Flycatcher is a common bird of scrub habitats in the western half of the state. It is part of a group of flycatchers that are very similar and hard to distinguish from one another.

37

White-throated Swift
Size: Length 6", Wingspan 13"

Summer range

Above & below: boldly patterned black & white
Wings: long, narrow
Tail: notched

D	R	I	K
K			B
I	N	G	

Box 6

Name the bird in box 6.

Cliff Swallow
Size: Length 6", Wingspan 12"

Summer range

Bulb-shaped nest

Above: dark
Below: whitish
Throat: dark orange or blackish
Cheeks: orange
Forehead: buff
Rump: orange
Tail: dark, stubby, square

Violet-green Swallow
Size: Length 6", Wingspan 13"

Summer range

Above: iridescent blue-green
Below: pure white
Tail: slightly forked
Flank patches: white which
nearly meet over the tail

©TPWPress 1997

┌─ Did You Know That . . .
The generic name for
the Chimney Swift,
Chaetura, means
"bristle-tail" in Greek.

Chimney Swift
Size: Length 5", Wingspan 12"

Summer range

Body: dark throughout
Tail: dark, stubby, square

Barn Swallow
Size: Length 7", Wingspan 13"

Summer range

Above: dark blue
Below: orange
Tail: dark, deeply forked

Swallows and Swifts

Although swallows and swifts look similar and both spend all of their time feeding on insects in mid-air, they are not very closely related. Swifts are actually more closely related to hummingbirds. Swallows belong with the songbird group and are more closely allied to flycatchers.

Blue Jay
Size: Length 11", Wingspan 16"

All year

Above: blue
Below: dirty white
Crest: blue
Neck: black
Wing: white bars
Tail tip: white

Steller's Jay
Size: Length 12", Wingspan 18"

All year

Head, chest & back: blackish
Throat, forehead & above the eye: streaked with white
Belly: bluish
Wings & tail: blue barred with black

©TPWPress 1997

— Did You Know That . . . —
Steller's Jay was named for the
German naturalist Georg
Steller, who accompanied the
explorer Vitus Bering on the
voyage during which what is
now known as the Bering Strait,
between Alaska and Siberia,
was discovered.

True or False?
A person who studies
birds is an ornithologist.

Western Scrub-Jay
Size: Length 11", Wingspan 13"

All year

Above: blue
Back: grayish
Throat: white with dark streaks
Breast: gray with dark streaks
Belly: gray
Cheeks & eyes: black with white
    border above

American Crow
Size: Length 18", Wingspan 36"

All year

Body: black throughout

Jays and Crows

Jays and crows are closely related. They are found all over the world, and Texas has 12 different species of these birds. In the eastern two-thirds of the state, the common jay is the Blue Jay. It is replaced in the west by the Western Scrub-Jay. Jays are very noisy, active birds that are easily attracted to bird feeders. Ravens and crows look much alike, but ravens have a heavier bill and a wedge-shaped tail.

If you were a bird, what would you look like?

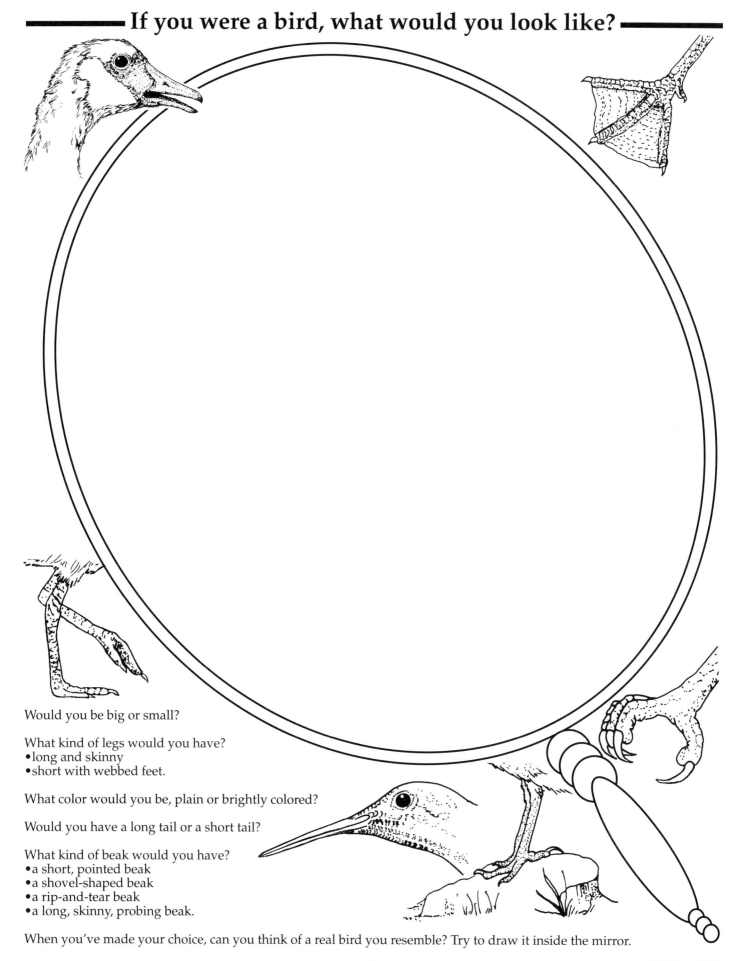

Would you be big or small?

What kind of legs would you have?
•long and skinny
•short with webbed feet.

What color would you be, plain or brightly colored?

Would you have a long tail or a short tail?

What kind of beak would you have?
•a short, pointed beak
•a shovel-shaped beak
•a rip-and-tear beak
•a long, skinny, probing beak.

When you've made your choice, can you think of a real bird you resemble? Try to draw it inside the mirror.

TPWPress 1997

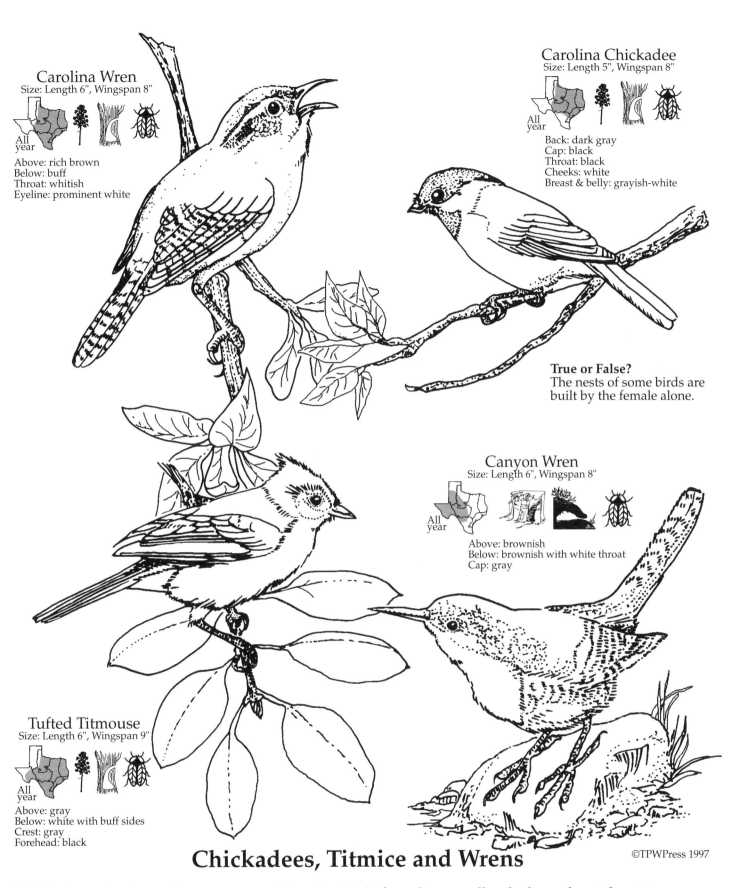

Carolina Wren
Size: Length 6", Wingspan 8"

All year

Above: rich brown
Below: buff
Throat: whitish
Eyeline: prominent white

Carolina Chickadee
Size: Length 5", Wingspan 8"

All year

Back: dark gray
Cap: black
Throat: black
Cheeks: white
Breast & belly: grayish-white

True or False?
The nests of some birds are
built by the female alone.

Canyon Wren
Size: Length 6", Wingspan 8"

All year

Above: brownish
Below: brownish with white throat
Cap: gray

Tufted Titmouse
Size: Length 6", Wingspan 9"

All year

Above: gray
Below: white with buff sides
Crest: gray
Forehead: black

Chickadees, Titmice and Wrens

Chickadees, titmice and wrens are small, active birds found in woodlands throughout the state. Tufted Titmice can be divided into two groups depending on the color of their crests; one group has black crests and the other has gray. The black-crested birds are found in the central and western parts of the state and the gray-crested birds are in the east. These two groups are sometimes considered separate species.

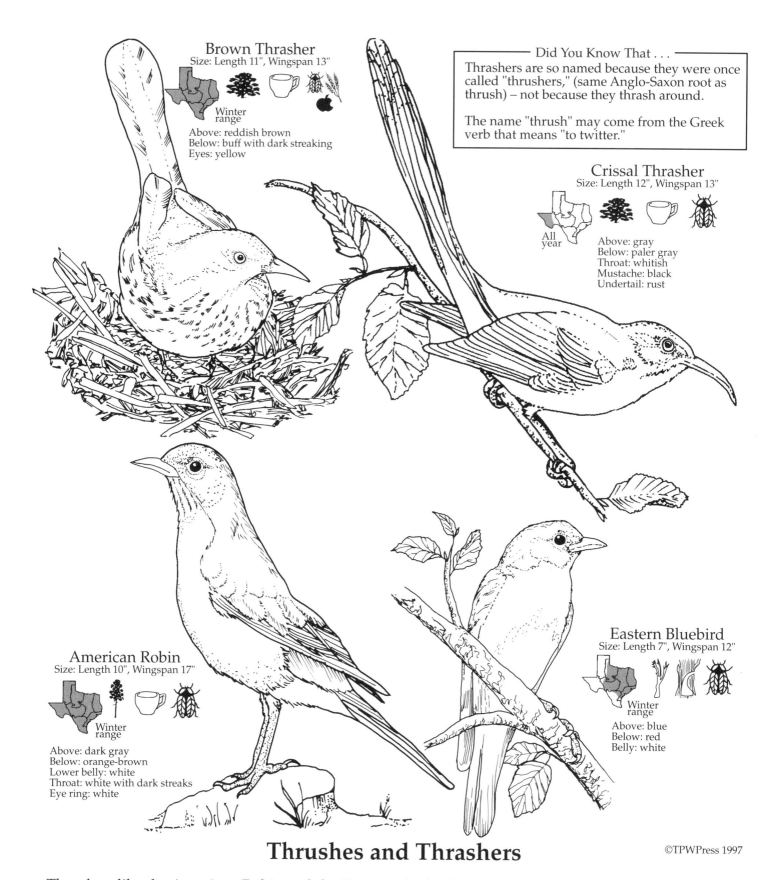

Brown Thrasher
Size: Length 11", Wingspan 13"

Winter range

Above: reddish brown
Below: buff with dark streaking
Eyes: yellow

Crissal Thrasher
Size: Length 12", Wingspan 13"

All year

Above: gray
Below: paler gray
Throat: whitish
Mustache: black
Undertail: rust

American Robin
Size: Length 10", Wingspan 17"

Winter range

Above: dark gray
Below: orange-brown
Lower belly: white
Throat: white with dark streaks
Eye ring: white

Eastern Bluebird
Size: Length 7", Wingspan 12"

Winter range

Above: blue
Below: red
Belly: white

Thrushes and Thrashers

©TPWPress 1997

Thrushes, like the American Robin and the Eastern Bluebird, are members of a very large family of birds. Most are wonderful songsters. All have relatively short narrow bills used for feeding on insects and fruit. Thrashers, which are also called mimic thrushes, belong to an entirely different bird family. Most have fairly long and thin curved bills. While thrushes are migratory, with many species spending their winter in Texas, mostly tropical thrashers do not migrate. Many, like the Northern Mockingbird (see page 15), mimic the song of other birds. Only a few species of thrashers are found in Texas.

42

Blue-headed (Solitary) Vireo
Size: Length 6", Wingspan 10"

Winter range

Back: greenish
Below: whitish with yellow flanks
Head: gray and white spectacles (lores, forehead & eye ring)
Rump: gray
Wing bars: white

Townsend's Warbler
Size: Length 5", Wingspan 8"

Spring and Fall migration

Above: greenish
Breast: yellow
Belly: white
Crown: black
Eye stripe: yellow
Ear stripe: black
Chin stripe: yellow
Throat: black
Wing bars: white

©TPWPress 1997

Wilson's Warbler
Size: Length 5", Wingspan 7"

Spring and Fall migration

Above: olive-yellow
Below: yellow
Cap: black (male)

Colima Warbler
Size: Length 5", Wingspan 8"

Summer range

Above: brownish-gray
Below: grayish-white with buff-brown flanks
Head: gray
Crown patch: reddish brown
Eye ring: white
Rump and undertail: orange-yellow

Vireos and Warblers

Most vireos and warblers are neotropical migrants. Some of these small birds travel all the way to South America during the winter, but some only come as far south as Texas. Warblers are usually brightly colored and very active, while vireos are dull in color and are more deliberate in their actions. The Colima Warbler is a Texas specialty. Even though most of its range is in Mexico, it is best known from Big Bend National Park in West Texas.

Pyrrhuloxia
Size: Length 9", Wingspan 12"

All year

Body: dusty gray
Crest & face: red
Belly, wings & tail: red

Rose-breasted Grosbeak
Size: Length 8", Wingspan 13"

Spring and Fall migration

Head, back, wings & tail: black
Breast: red
Belly & rump: white
Wing patches & tail spots: white
Underwing: red

─── Did You Know That. . . ───
The root of the word "indigo" in
Indigo Bunting is the same as
"Indian." Both words refer to India,
the subcontinent that is the source of
the bluish plant dye called indigo.

Lazuli Bunting
Size: Length 6", Wingspan 9"

Spring and Fall migration

Head, rump & back: turquoise
Breast: rust
Belly: buff
Wing bars: white

Indigo Bunting
Size: Length 6", Wingspan 9"

Spring and Fall migration

Body: indigo blue throughout

Grosbeaks and Buntings

©TPWPress 1997

Grosbeaks and tropical buntings are a small group of brightly-colored seed-eating birds. Most of the
birds in this group form species pairs that are separated by the Great Plains. That is to say, one species
is found west of the Great Plains and the other, east of the Great Plains. Such birds once probably
belonged to a single species that became separated into two populations when the plains first formed
after the Ice Ages. The two groups then changed to form distinct species. The Indigo and Lazuli
Buntings form one of these species pairs.

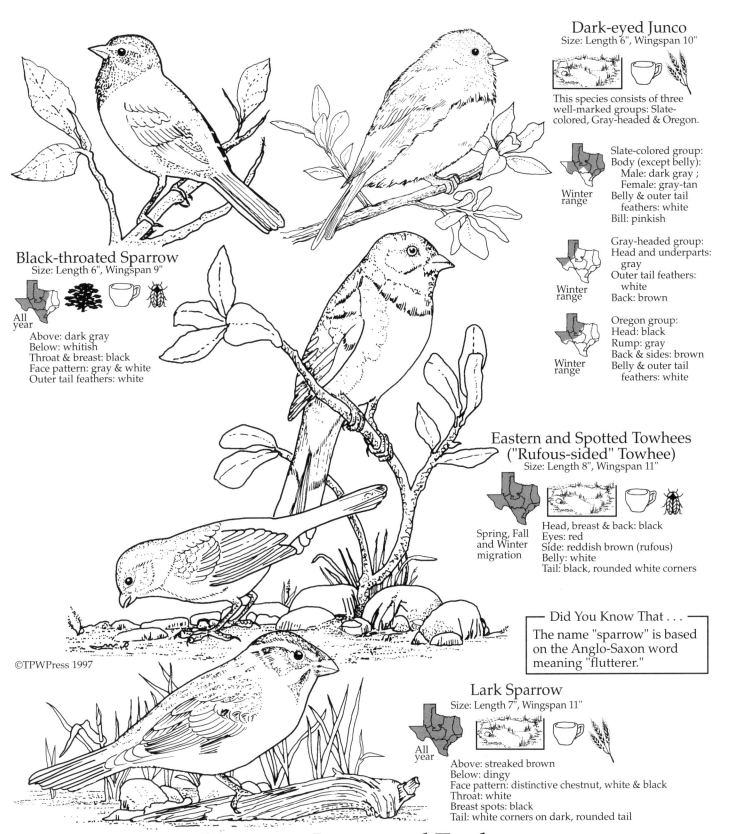

Dark-eyed Junco
Size: Length 6", Wingspan 10"

This species consists of three well-marked groups: Slate-colored, Gray-headed & Oregon.

Winter range
Slate-colored group:
Body (except belly):
  Male: dark gray ;
  Female: gray-tan
Belly & outer tail
  feathers: white
Bill: pinkish

Winter range
Gray-headed group:
Head and underparts:
  gray
Outer tail feathers:
  white
Back: brown

Winter range
Oregon group:
Head: black
Rump: gray
Back & sides: brown
Belly & outer tail
  feathers: white

Black-throated Sparrow
Size: Length 6", Wingspan 9"

All year
Above: dark gray
Below: whitish
Throat & breast: black
Face pattern: gray & white
Outer tail feathers: white

Eastern and Spotted Towhees ("Rufous-sided" Towhee)
Size: Length 8", Wingspan 11"

Spring, Fall and Winter migration
Head, breast & back: black
Eyes: red
Side: reddish brown (rufous)
Belly: white
Tail: black, rounded white corners

┌─ Did You Know That . . .
The name "sparrow" is based on the Anglo-Saxon word meaning "flutterer."

©TPWPress 1997

Lark Sparrow
Size: Length 7", Wingspan 11"

All year
Above: streaked brown
Below: dingy
Face pattern: distinctive chestnut, white & black
Throat: white
Breast spots: black
Tail: white corners on dark, rounded tail

Sparrows, Juncos and Towhees

Many different kinds of sparrows and the related Dark-eyed Junco and "Rufous-sided" Towhee are common throughout the United States, and Texas is the wintering ground for many of them. Most sparrows are brown, but on close inspection have very intricate and beautiful plumages. The common House Sparrow is not actually related to these birds, it is an Old World Sparrow that has been introduced from Europe.

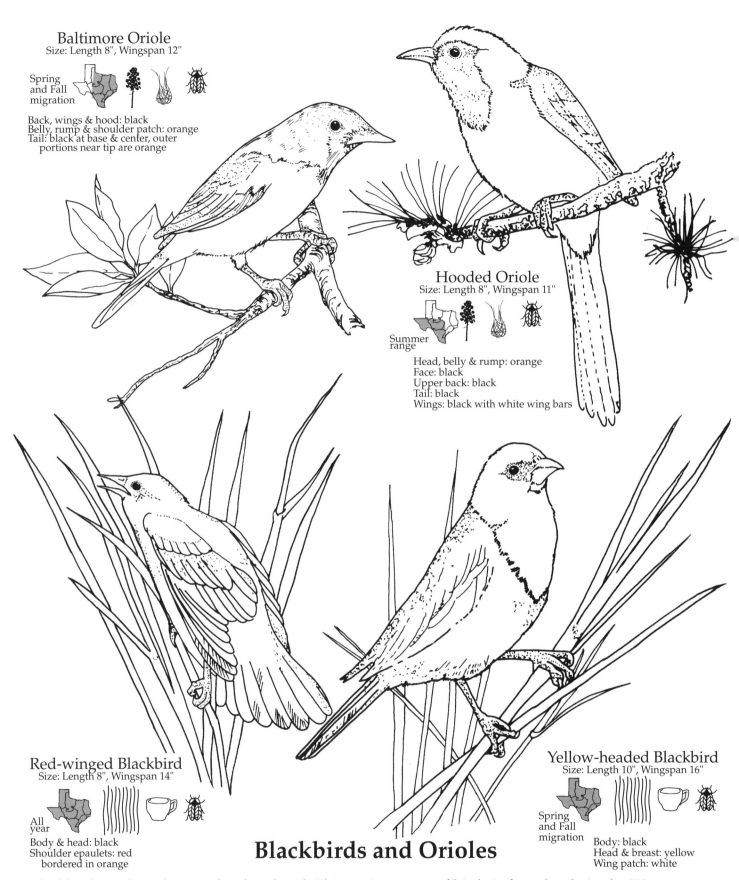

Baltimore Oriole
Size: Length 8", Wingspan 12"

Spring and Fall migration

Back, wings & hood: black
Belly, rump & shoulder patch: orange
Tail: black at base & center, outer portions near tip are orange

Hooded Oriole
Size: Length 8", Wingspan 11"

Summer range

Head, belly & rump: orange
Face: black
Upper back: black
Tail: black
Wings: black with white wing bars

Red-winged Blackbird
Size: Length 8", Wingspan 14"

All year

Body & head: black
Shoulder epaulets: red bordered in orange

Yellow-headed Blackbird
Size: Length 10", Wingspan 16"

Spring and Fall migration

Body: black
Head & breast: yellow
Wing patch: white

Blackbirds and Orioles

Blackbirds and orioles are closely related. This entire group of birds is found only in the Western Hemisphere or New World. True blackbirds are found nowhere else. Some of the birds in this group, the cowbirds, are brood parasites. They lay their eggs in other birds' nests and let those birds raise the young cowbirds. This is a threat to some rare birds because they end up raising too many cowbirds and not enough of their own young.

Build A Paper Birdhouse

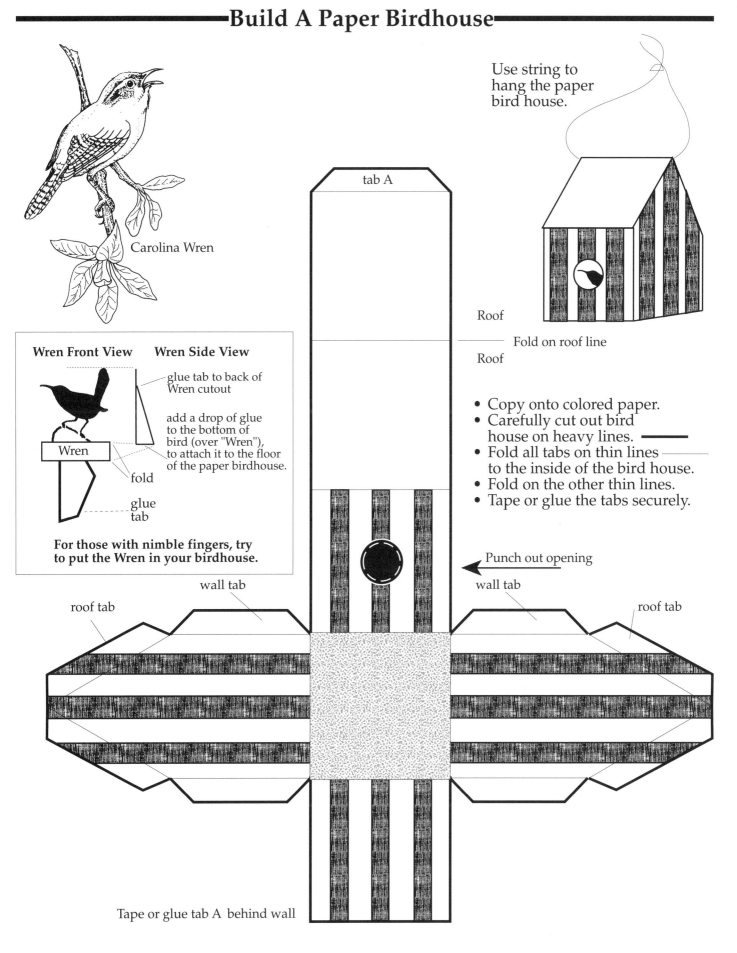

Carolina Wren

Use string to hang the paper bird house.

tab A

Roof

Fold on roof line

Roof

- Copy onto colored paper.
- Carefully cut out bird house on heavy lines. ▬▬
- Fold all tabs on thin lines ───── to the inside of the bird house.
- Fold on the other thin lines.
- Tape or glue the tabs securely.

Wren Front View   Wren Side View

glue tab to back of Wren cutout

add a drop of glue to the bottom of bird (over "Wren"), to attach it to the floor of the paper birdhouse.

Wren

fold

glue tab

For those with nimble fingers, try to put the Wren in your birdhouse.

roof tab

wall tab

Punch out opening

wall tab

roof tab

Tape or glue tab A behind wall

True or False
Pages 5, 9, 12, 13, 17, 25, 26, 39, 41.
All answers are TRUE.

Actions of the Feet, page 13

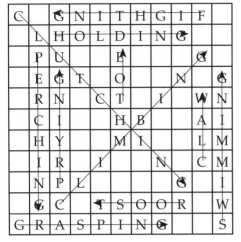

SWIMMING
PRYING
FIGHTING
PERCHING
CLIMBING
CLUTCHING
HOLDING
GRASPING
ROOSTING
CLAWING

The Actions of the Bill, page 15

GRASPING
CARRYING
SCRATCHING
DIGGING
CRACKING
CATCHING
EATING
CUTTING
HATCHING
CLIMBING
EGG TURNING

IF YOU SEE A FEEDING BIRD OBSERVE ITS BEHAVIOR.

Box 3, page 16
WARBLERS

W	A	R
S		B
R	E	L

Box 4, page 17
CARDINAL

N	A	L
I		C
D	R	A

Page 18

Scissor-tailed
Flycatcher

Mourning
Dove

Box 1, page 13
KILLDEER

L	L	I
D		K
E	E	R

Bird Scrabble, page 28

1	MOCKINGBIRD	6	ROADRUNNER
2	KILLDEER	7	BUNTING
3	HERON	8	HAWK
4	OWL	9	CARDINAL
5	KINGFISHER	10	FLYCATCHER

Box 2, page 15
BLUEBIRD

U	L	B
E		D
B	I	R

Box 5, page 37
THRASHER

S	H	E
A		R
R	H	T

Box 6, page 38
KINGBIRD

D	R	I
	K	B
	I	N	G

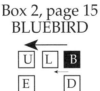

Texas Birds

The following is a list of bird species either accepted for Texas by the Texas Bird Records Committee (TBRC) of the Texas Ornithological Society or those species recently documented that are expected to be accepted. This list totals 612 species as of August 1997 and includes taxonomic and nomenclatural changes outlined in the 41st supplement (Auk, July 1997) to the AOU Check-list of North American Birds.

I = Introduced (6)
E = Extinct (3)
u = uncertain origin (stable to increasing populations of introduced/native origin) (2)
* = birds expected to be accepted by the TBRC (8)

LOONS (Order Gaviiformes, Family Gaviidae)
Red-throated Loon
Pacific Loon
Common Loon
Yellow-billed Loon

GREBES (Order Podicipediformes, Family Podicipedidae)
Least Grebe
Pied-billed Grebe
Horned Grebe
Red-necked Grebe
Eared Grebe
Western Grebe
Clark's Grebe

ALBATROSSES Order Procellariiformes, Family Diomedeiidae)
Yellow-nosed Albatross

SHEARWATERS AND PETRELS (Order Procellariiformes, Family Procellariidae)
White-chinned Petrel
Black-capped Petrel *
Cory's Shearwater
Greater Shearwater
Sooty Shearwater
Manx Shearwater
Audubon's Shearwater

STORM-PETRELS (Order Procellariiformes, Family Hydrobatidae)
Wilson's Storm-Petrel
Leach's Storm-Petrel
Band-rumped Storm-Petrel

TROPICBIRDS (Order Pelecaniformes, Family Phaethontidae)
Red-billed Tropicbird

BOOBIES AND GANNETS (Order Pelecaniformes, Family Sulidae)
Masked Booby
Blue-footed Booby
Brown Booby
Red-footed Booby
Northern Gannet

PELICANS (Order Pelecaniformes, Family Pelicanidae)
American White Pelican
Brown Pelican

CORMORANTS (Order Pelecaniformes, Family Phalacrocoracidae)
Double-crested Cormorant
Neotropic Cormorant

DARTERS (Order Pelecaniformes, Family Anhingidae)
Anhinga

FRIGATEBIRDS (Order Pelecaniformes, Family Fregatidae)
Magnificent Frigatebird

BITTERNS AND HERONS (Order Ciconiiformes, Family Ardeidae)
American Bittern
Least Bittern
Great Blue Heron
Great Egret
Snowy Egret
Little Blue Heron
Tricolored Heron
Reddish Egret
Cattle Egret
Green Heron
Black-crowned Night-Heron
Yellow-crowned Night-Heron

IBISES AND SPOONBILLS (Order Ciconiiformes, Family Threskiornithidae)
White Ibis
Glossy Ibis
White-faced Ibis
Roseate Spoonbill

STORKS (Order Ciconiiformes, Family Ciconiidae)
Jabiru
Wood Stork

AMERICAN VULTURES (Order Ciconiiformes, Family Cathartidae)
Black Vulture
Turkey Vulture

FLAMINGOES (Order Phoenicopteriformes, Family Phoenicopteridae)
Greater Flamingo

SWANS, GEESE AND DUCKS (Order Anseriformes, Family Anatidae)
Black-bellied Whistling-Duck
Fulvous Whistling-Duck
Greater White-fronted Goose
Snow Goose
Ross's Goose
Canada Goose
Brant
Trumpeter Swan
Tundra Swan
Muscovy Duck
Wood Duck
Gadwall
Eurasian Wigeon
American Wigeon
American Black Duck
Mallard
Mottled Duck
Blue-winged Teal
Cinnamon Teal
Northern Shoveler
White-cheeked Pintail
Northern Pintail
Garganey
Green-winged Teal
Canvasback
Redhead
Ring-necked Duck
Greater Scaup
Lesser Scaup
Harlequin Duck
Surf Scoter
White-winged Scoter
Black Scoter
Oldsquaw
Bufflehead
Common Goldeneye
Barrow's Goldeneye
Hooded Merganser
Red-breasted Merganser
Common Merganser
Masked Duck
Ruddy Duck

KITES, HAWKS, EAGLES AND ALLIES (Order Falconiformes, Family Accipitridae)
Osprey
Hook-billed Kite
Swallow-tailed Kite
White-tailed Kite
Snail Kite
Mississippi Kite
Bald Eagle
Northern Harrier
Sharp-shinned Hawk
Cooper's Hawk
Northern Goshawk
Crane Hawk
Gray Hawk
Common Black-Hawk
Harris's Hawk
Roadside Hawk
Red-shouldered Hawk
Broad-winged Hawk
Short-tailed Hawk
Swainson's Hawk
White-tailed Hawk
Zone-tailed Hawk
Red-tailed Hawk
Ferruginous Hawk
Rough-legged Hawk
Golden Eagle

CARACARAS AND FALCONS (Order Falconiformes, Family Falconidae)
Crested Caracara
Collared Forest-Falcon
American Kestrel
Merlin
Aplomado Falcon
Prairie Falcon
Peregrine Falcon

GUANS (Order Galliformes, Family Cracidae)
Plain Chachalaca

PHEASANTS, GROUSE AND TURKEYS (Order Galliformes, Family Phasianiidae)
Ring-necked Pheasant (I)
Greater Prairie-Chicken
Lesser Prairie-Chicken
Wild Turkey

NEW WORLD QUAIL (Order Galliformes, Family Odontophoridae)
Montezuma Quail
Northern Bobwhite
Scaled Quail
Gambel's Quail

RAILS, GALLINULES AND COOTS (Order Gruiformes, Family Rallidae)
Yellow Rail
Black Rail
Clapper Rail
King Rail
Virginia Rail
Sora
Paint-billed Crake
Spotted Rail
Purple Gallinule
Common Moorhen
American Coot

CRANES (Order Gruiformes, Family Gruidae)
Sandhill Crane
Whooping Crane

THICK-KNEES (Order Charadriiformes, Family Burhinidae)
Double-striped Thick-knee

PLOVERS (Order Charadriiformes, Family Charadriidae)
Black-bellied Plover
American Golden-Plover
Collared Plover
Snowy Plover
Wilson's Plover
Semipalmated Plover
Piping Plover
Killdeer
Mountain Plover

OYSTERCATCHERS (Order Charadriiformes, Family Haematopodidae)
American Oystercatcher

STILTS AND AVOCETS (Order Charadriiformes, Family Recurvirostridae)
Black-necked Stilt
American Avocet

JACANAS (Order Charadriiformes, Family Jacanidae)
Northern Jacana

SANDPIPERS AND ALLIES (Order Charadriiformes, Family Scolopacidae)
Greater Yellowlegs
Lesser Yellowlegs
Solitary Sandpiper
Willet
Wandering Tattler
Spotted Sandpiper
Upland Sandpiper
Eskimo Curlew
Whimbrel
Long-billed Curlew
Hudsonian Godwit
Marbled Godwit
Ruddy Turnstone
Surfbird
Red Knot
Sanderling
Semipalmated Sandpiper
Western Sandpiper
Red-necked Stint
Least Sandpiper
White-rumped Sandpiper
Baird's Sandpiper
Pectoral Sandpiper
Sharp-tailed Sandpiper
Purple Sandpiper
Dunlin
Curlew Sandpiper
Stilt Sandpiper
Buff-breasted Sandpiper
Ruff
Short-billed Dowitcher
Long-billed Dowitcher
Common Snipe
American Woodcock
Wilson's Phalarope
Red-necked Phalarope
Red Phalarope

GULLS, TERNS AND SKIMMERS (Order Charadriiformes, Family Laridae)
Pomarine Jaeger
Parasitic Jaeger
Long-tailed Jaeger
Laughing Gull
Franklin's Gull
Little Gull
Black-headed Gull
Bonaparte's Gull
Heermann's Gull
Mew Gull
Ring-billed Gull
California Gull
Herring Gull
Thayer's Gull
Iceland Gull
Lesser Black-backed Gull
Slaty-backed Gull
Western Gull
Glaucous Gull
Great Black-backed Gull
Kelp Gull
Black-legged Kittiwake
Sabine's Gull
Gull-billed Tern
Caspian Tern
Royal Tern
Elegant Tern
Sandwich Tern
Roseate Tern *
Common Tern
Arctic Tern *
Forster's Tern
Least Tern
Bridled Tern
Sooty Tern
Black Tern
Brown Noddy
Black Noddy
Black Skimmer

PIGEONS AND DOVES (Order Columbiformes, Family Columbidae)
Rock Dove (I)
Red-billed Pigeon
Band-tailed Pigeon
Eurasian Collared-Dove (I)*
White-winged Dove
Mourning Dove
Passenger Pigeon (E)
Inca Dove
Common Ground-Dove
Ruddy Ground-Dove
Ruddy Quail-Dove
White-tipped Dove

PARAKEETS AND PARROTS (Order Psittaciformes, Family Psittacidae)
Monk Parakeet (I)
Carolina Parakeet (E)
Green Parakeet (u)
Red-crowned Parrot (u)

CUCKOOS, ROADRUNNERS AND ANIS (Order Cuculiformes, Family Cuculidae)
Black-billed Cuckoo
Yellow-billed Cuckoo
Mangrove Cuckoo
Greater Roadrunner
Groove-billed Ani

BARN OWLS (Order Strigiformes, Family Tytonidae)
Barn Owl

TYPICAL OWLS (Order Strigiformes, Family Strigidae)
Flammulated Owl
Eastern Screech-Owl
Western Screech-Owl
Great Horned Owl
Snowy Owl
Northern Pygmy-Owl
Ferruginous Pygmy-Owl
Elf Owl
Burrowing Owl
Mottled Owl
Spotted Owl
Barred Owl
Long-eared Owl
Stygian Owl *
Short-eared Owl
Northern Saw-whet Owl

NIGHTJARS (Order Caprimulgiformes, Family Caprimulgidae)
Lesser Nighthawk
Common Nighthawk
Pauraque
Common Poorwill
Chuck-will's-widow
Whip-poor-will

SWIFTS (Order Apodiformes, Family Apodidae)
White-collared Swift
Chimney Swift
White-throated Swift

HUMMINGBIRDS (Order Apodiformes, Family Trochilidae)
Green Violet-ear
Green-breasted Mango
Broad-billed Hummingbird
White-eared Hummingbird
Berylline Hummingbird *
Buff-bellied Hummingbird
Violet-crowned Hummingbird
Blue-throated Hummingbird
Magnificent Hummingbird
Lucifer Hummingbird
Ruby-throated Hummingbird
Black-chinned Hummingbird
Anna's Hummingbird
Costa's Hummingbird
Calliope Hummingbird
Broad-tailed Hummingbird
Rufous Hummingbird
Allen's Hummingbird

TROGONS (Order Trogoniformes, Family Trogonidae)
Elegant Trogon

KINGFISHERS (Order Coraciiformes, Family Alcedinidae)
Ringed Kingfisher
Belted Kingfisher
Green Kingfisher

WOODPECKERS AND ALLIES (Order Piciformes, Family Picidae)
Lewis's Woodpecker
Red-headed Woodpecker
Acorn Woodpecker
Golden-fronted Woodpecker
Red-bellied Woodpecker
Yellow-bellied Sapsucker
Red-naped Sapsucker
Red-breasted Sapsucker *
Williamson's Sapsucker
Ladder-backed Woodpecker
Downy Woodpecker
Hairy Woodpecker
Red-cockaded Woodpecker
Northern Flicker
Pileated Woodpecker
Ivory-billed Woodpecker (E)

TYRANT FLYCATCHERS (Order Passeriformes, Family Tyrannidae)
Northern Beardless-Tyrannulet
Greenish Elaenia
Tufted Flycatcher
Olive-sided Flycatcher
Greater Pewee
Western Wood-Pewee
Eastern Wood-Pewee
Yellow-bellied Flycatcher
Acadian Flycatcher
Alder Flycatcher
Willow Flycatcher
Least Flycatcher
Hammond's Flycatcher
Dusky Flycatcher
Gray Flycatcher
Cordilleran Flycatcher
Black Phoebe
Eastern Phoebe
Say's Phoebe
Vermilion Flycatcher
Dusky-capped Flycatcher
Ash-throated Flycatcher
Great Crested Flycatcher
Brown-crested Flycatcher
Great Kiskadee
Sulphur-bellied Flycatcher
Tropical Kingbird
Couch's Kingbird
Cassin's Kingbird
Thick-billed Kingbird
Western Kingbird
Eastern Kingbird
Gray Kingbird
Scissor-tailed Flycatcher
Fork-tailed Flycatcher
Rose-throated Becard
Masked Tityra

SHRIKES (Order Passeriformes, Family Laniidae)
Northern Shrike
Loggerhead Shrike

VIREOS (Order Passeriformes, Family Vireonidae)
White-eyed Vireo
Bell's Vireo
Black-capped Vireo
Gray Vireo
Blue-headed (Solitary) Vireo
Cassin's (Solitary) Vireo
Plumbeous (Solitary) Vireo
Yellow-throated Vireo
Hutton's Vireo
Warbling Vireo
Philadelphia Vireo
Red-eyed Vireo
Yellow-green Vireo
Black-whiskered Vireo
Yucatan Vireo

JAYS, MAGPIES AND CROWS (Order Passeriformes, Family Corvidae)
Steller's Jay
Blue Jay
Green Jay
Brown Jay
Western Scrub-Jay
Mexican Jay
Pinyon Jay
Clark's Nutcracker
Black-billed Magpie
American Crow
Tamaulipas Crow
Fish Crow
Chihuahuan Raven
Common Raven

LARKS (Order Passeriformes, Family Alaudidae)
Horned Lark

SWALLOWS (Order Passeriformes, Family Hirundinidae)
Purple Martin
Gray-breasted Martin
Tree Swallow
Violet-green Swallow
Northern Rough-winged Swallow
Bank Swallow
Barn Swallow
Cliff Swallow
Cave Swallow

TITMICE (Order Passeriformes, Family Paridae)
Carolina Chickadee
Black-capped Chickadee
Mountain Chickadee
Juniper (Plain) Titmouse
Tufted Titmouse

VERDINS (Order Passeriformes, Family Remizidae)
Verdin

BUSHTITS (Order Passeriformes, Family Aegithalidae)
Bushtit

NUTHATCHES (Order Passeriformes, Family Sittidae)
Red-breasted Nuthatch
White-breasted Nuthatch
Pygmy Nuthatch
Brown-headed Nuthatch

CREEPERS (Order Passeriformes, Family Certhiidae)
Brown Creeper

WRENS (Order Passeriformes, Family Troglodytidae)
Cactus Wren
Rock Wren
Canyon Wren
Carolina Wren
Bewick's Wren
House Wren
Winter Wren
Sedge Wren
Marsh Wren

DIPPERS (Order Passeriformes, Family Cinclidae)
American Dipper

KINGLETS (Order Passeriformes, Family Regulidae)
Golden-crowned Kinglet
Ruby-crowned Kinglet